FLOOD STAGE

When Revival Takes Over

Randall E. Burton

B&B PUBLISHING GROUP

ISBN: 9798368381060

"As a follow up to his powerful book, River Rising, my good friend Randall Burton has penned this provocative and challenging call to every believer to dive deeper into the Spirit of God. His unquenchable thirst for the things of God will stir and provoke the thirst of any reader. At no point in the book does Randall give the impression that he has arrived or that he has all of the answers. He simply invites each of us on a journey beyond our personal place of comfort and familiarity.

If you are content in your walk in the Spirit, then this book may not be for you. But if you are willing to dive in deeper, then make sure to read the pages again and again until you are in waters that no man can cross."

Rodney Burton
Minister & Author
www.rodneyburton.net

"Convicting and passionate truth. In his new book Flood Stage, Pastor Randall Burton discusses the soon coming revival. He addresses the church's need to be prepared for this mighty end-time revival. Furthermore, Burton outlines the necessities of navigating a move of God, providing essential insight for any novice seeker or seasoned revivalist."

Jordan Cunnington,
Redemption Project Ministries
www.redemptionprojectinc.org

"Apostle Randall Burton is a much-needed voice to the American Church and to the nations. With clarity and practicality, he is calling the church back to a place of hungering for the glory of God and for revival. As you read Flood Stage, let it whet your appetite for more of God. May

the nations be flooded with God's glory in the name of Jesus."
Lydia Marrow
Vanguard Ministries
www.vanguardministries.tv

"Once again, my friend Randall Burton has written yet another extension from his revelation about God's river. His newly released book, <u>Flood Stage,</u> guides the reader deeper into the move of God taking place now on the earth. Building from and on the dynamics of his book, <u>River Rising</u>, Pastor Randall sets a course that takes the reader immediately into a deeper understanding of God's Presence, as he uses personal experiences, biblical teaching, and powerful prophetic insight to launch the reader out into God's flowing waters of outpouring.

Thank you, Pastor/Apostle Randall, for once again penning a tool to help every reader navigate God's river, rising at <u>Flood Stage</u>."
Keith E. Taylor Senior Pastor Cross Tabernacle Church, Terre Haute, Indiana. Founder and CEO of Gilgal Ministries Inc.

"There is a reason why true revival tarries, and my Apostolic friend, Randall Burton, unpacks some of the reasons why. This book is a must read if you are serious about positioning yourself for the greatest outpouring the world has ever seen. Well done, Randall."
Graham Renouf
Prophet/Pastor
Lower Hutt New Zealand

"When Randall Burton asked me to write an endorsement for Flood Stage, I was both honored and excited. Honored that my opinion might matter. Excited because I have watched the journey in his life and church for over a twelve-year period of time. I knew the genuine nature of the move of God on that journey. As I wrote in endorsing his first book, Randall had not only experienced a move of God, but he actually was learning the principles of sustaining it. In this book he shares principles that have taken the church past the river stage and to the flood stage. Once again, he shows he actually understands what he is talking about. While every pastor would benefit from this book, it is not just a book for pastors.

Most of it is directly applicable to the individual. He contends that church revival and national revival will never go higher than personal revival. Your personal revival is necessary and is planned by heaven. Some are always looking to expose hidden secrets. Well, Randall devotes a chapter to revealing the secret ingredients to revival. His final key is...well I will let you read it... but I will tell you it is powerful. Chapter eight deals with purpose and pollution. Don't miss this chapter. I think chapter ten, on "Flow," is worth the purchase of the entire book. I love this quote, "Some have marveled at the team approach in which my fivefold ministry friends demonstrate as we flow together during ministry gatherings...[and]...have demonstrated unselfish submission as we move with God in real time" If chapter eleven does not produce shouting ground for you then you need more than revival. You probably need resurrection! In chapter twelve he describes the importance of being "drenched." After quoting Smith Wigglesworth and William Seymour he explores transformation. Real world results follow an encounter with the glory. If you want to go past dabbling your toe In the river, you will find this book helpful!"

Michael Livengood
Doorkeepers International
USA/New Zealand
www.mikelivengoodministries.com

"Throughout church history many have tried to define, manufacture, pattern, and produce revival. Nearly all of them have failed. Why? You cannot strive yourself into a move of God. Self-effort will not force God's hand. Today, there is currently a great cry for revival. In this nation, there are many opinions on what revival is or isn't. In "Flood Stage" Randall Burton has captured the essence of revival.

"Flood Stage" will not only deepen your knowledge of what a true move of God is, but it will ignite a desire within you to see the flames of revival spread across the earth. I feel this book would make a wonderful textbook for a course on revival as it is well written and filled with valuable insight and teachings. If you are hungry for the presence of God, I encourage you to read "Flood Stage."

James Cowan
J110 Ministries
www.j110ministries.com

"I have known Randall Burton for over a decade and have ministered alongside him. I have read almost every work he has written, yet this is by far his most thought-provoking book to date! In this book, he covers the blessings and pitfalls of revival, the ingredients necessary to sustain revival, the cost of revival, the problems encountered in a move of God, and more.

Having known Randall and having been involved in the move of God within the walls of the Church he Pastors, I have to state that he is more than qualified to speak on this subject. He has been the Pastor/Apostle of a sustained and ever-increasing move of God for more than eleven years in his Church.

In the tenth chapter of this book, he makes a statement worth paying attention to; **"Friends, we are in a time when the river of God's presence is coming on the earth like a flood. You will either be caught up in the rising tide of His glory or you will be washed away in the flow of His raging waters."**

Believe me, I have read this book two times and scanned through it a third time; I have over thirteen type-written pages of notes! Every Pastor and individual who is hungry for Revival needs to read this book and then read it again!

My favorite chapters are 2-12; however, you must read chapter one to get ready for the rest of the book. Hear me, there are many thought-provoking statements throughout this book such as:

"Some people who are saved, filled with the Spirit and possess the gifts of heaven may in fact not go to heaven!"

"The church does not lack the reproductive organs to multiply the kingdom of God, what the church lacks is intimacy with the bridegroom. The less time we spend with the bridegroom the less our chances of being impregnated with his will for our lives becomes."

I could go on and on but then if I did, I would be writing a book within a book! I encourage you to not only purchase a copy of this book for yourself, but gift a book to your Pastor or leader".

Fredrick R. Aguilar
Fire on the Altar Ministries
Zion, Illinois

INTRODUCTION

The Far-Reaching Rivers of Life

In his book, My Utmost For His Highest, Oswald Chambers writes, "A river is victoriously persistent, overcoming all barriers. For a while it goes steadily on its course, but then comes back to an obstacle. And for a while it is blocked, yet it soon makes a pathway around the obstacle. Or a river will drop out of sight for miles, only later to emerge again even broader and greater than ever."

It has been seven years since we released the book, River Rising, to the world. It is a book which chronicles the beginning stages of a move of God that began in my heart nearly twelve years ago. It has impacted the lives of ministers, churches and people from around the world. What we have learned since then is that there are no lifeguards on the riverbank, no expert swimmers in the rapid flowing waters of revival, only adventurers who throw caution to the wind and dive right in. When the river of God is flowing, there is always a current.

I've heard it said since the days of my personal pentecostal experience in 1982 that "there is coming a revival such as the world has yet to see." Though I've read the books and articles about revivals, heard the stories and have been in some very special moves of God myself, I have yet to see or hear about this be-all

1

and end-all revival. I emphasize the word yet because even though we haven't seen it, it doesn't mean that it's not coming.

The word river occurs 148 times in the King James Version Bible and the word rivers is found in 71 places. More important to the subject matter in this book, the word flood occurs 39 different times in scripture. Flood stage is the level at which a body of water's surface has risen to a sufficient level to cause inundation of areas that are not normally covered by water, causing an inconvenience or a threat to life and/or property.

This book is a tribute to a God who honors His word and the obedience of His servants who are willing to risk it all to follow Him. As you read its pages, my prayer is that the flood stage of His glory causes an insatiable thirst for more of God in your life. Are you ready for it? He's ready to do it!

CHAPTER 1

The Great Flood

Isaiah 43:2: "When you pass through the waters, I will be with you; And through the rivers, they shall not overflow you."

It began on the evening of June 6, 2008. Rain began to fill the sky over central Indiana. By the end of the next day, thunderstorms produced heavy rains in the amount of twelve inches in some portions of our county. ¹During the peak of this deluge, the river crested at a record stage of 18.61 feet. The east fork of the White River flowed at 68,100 cubic feet per second! Two levees and a dam upstream were breached as the waters flooded our beautiful city.

This great flood in Columbus, Indiana, caused a tremendous amount of property damage and the lives of many to be disrupted for months afterward. As many as 3000 residents were displaced after the waters had receded. As the rains came down and the flood engulfed our city, we were cut off from the outside world and for several weeks following we were living in a veritable stone-age. At our local hospital, 157 patients had to be evacuated, as 130 million gallons of water poured into the basement and shut it down for over four months. Businesses were emptied out and emergency shelters were full of stunned residents. My heart still breaks as I think of the disruption and despair that this flood caused to so many wonderful people in our city. Columbus, Indiana, is a beautiful city which takes great pride in its architecture, diversity and now in its preparedness for a catastrophic flood.

In the aftermath of this flood, the usual agencies came in to help dig us out of this catastrophe: the Red Cross, Convoy of Hope and Operation Blessing, to name a few. Our church played a small part in reaching out and ministering to the people of our community during this difficult time, but it seemed like we were spitting into the wind because of the devastation caused by the flood waters.

Since that fateful day, our city has recovered, and we have learned a few things from this flood. We have worked on our waterways, reinforced our levees and drainage systems. In the event of another flood such as the one in 2008, we are far more prepared to deal with the rising rivers that run through and around our town. Yet every time we have some minor flooding in our city, some of us get a bit restless.

Just a few thousand years before the great flood in Columbus, Indiana, there was another great flood which is recorded in the Bible. At that time the earth was full of sin because man had strayed away from God. Sin had gotten so bad that God repented that he made men (Genesis 6:6). Because of this, the wrath of God was unstoppable. Thankfully, there was a man by the name of Noah, who was a righteous man, who believed and served God. The scripture says in Genesis 6:9 that Noah was a just man, perfect in his generation, and by generations we are speaking of God's righteousness being imputed into him. It goes on to say that, "Noah walked with God." That may not mean much to you today but consider that Noah was 600 years old when God flooded the earth. That's quite a track record of faithfulness, if you ask me. Genesis

6:8 says that "... Noah found grace in the eyes of the Lord." Grace simply means favor with God. I suppose that when you are walking with the Lord every day for 600 years, and you are able to look into His eyes each day, that's where you will find His grace. Noah had a deep, intimate relationship with God. Our perfection is found in our ability to lock eyes with God on a daily basis.

God speaks directly to Noah about the upcoming apocalypse that was coming upon the earth in the form of a flood. In Genesis 6:14 God says to Noah, "Make yourself an ark of gopherwood..." Then God gives him further details by telling him in verse 17, "And behold I Myself am bringing floodwaters on the earth, to destroy from under heaven all flesh in which is the breath of life; everything that is on the earth shall die."

What a downer, or should I say, "drowner." That is not good news. If you read just one more verse, you will find hope. In Genesis 6:18 God says, "But I will establish my covenant with you; and you shall go into the ark--you, your sons, your wife, and your sons' wives with you." God says to Noah, "I will establish my covenant with you..."

Noah's name means rest, and for many years Noah lived at peace with God while the world around him sank further and further in a downward spiral. The apocalyptic flood eventually happened as the rains poured down and the deep gave up its waters, that the Ark lifted off the ground and Noah and his family were thrown into a state of unrest (Genesis 7:17-24).

For forty days and forty nights they were tossed about at the mercy of God in a flood stage. As you read the rest of the story, you'll note that God makes good on His promises by flooding the earth and destroying all living flesh, but it was Noah and his family that were saved.

For those of you who may doubt the flood story in Genesis, you need to know that there are similar stories of this flood found in ancient texts from all over the world. And I found that in one study, ²that there is enough water in the oceans right now to cover the earth 8,000 feet deep if the surface of the earth were smooth. There is far too much evidence that points to this cataclysmic historical flood in Noah's days that should relieve doubt in today's well educated scientific world.

The great news is that God vowed never to flood the earth again as it happened in Noah's days. But I believe that one of the reasons for this was that as soon as Noah got off the boat and touched soil again, he built an altar before the Lord and made a sacrifice to God (Genesis 8:20-21). Then God follows up with Noah in Genesis 9:1 by saying; "...Be fruitful and multiply and fill the earth." It was at this point that God revealed His true heart to Noah by establishing His covenant through doing something that had never been seen before, until that day.

On that day, God sent a rainbow in the sky as a sign of peace between He and His new world.

Genesis 9:13-17: "I set My rainbow in the cloud, and it shall be for the sign of the covenant between Me and the earth. 14 It shall be, when I bring a cloud over the earth, that the rainbow shall be seen in the cloud; 15 and I will remember My covenant which is between Me and you and every living creature of all flesh; the waters shall never again become a flood to destroy all flesh. 16 The rainbow shall be in the cloud, and I will look on it to remember the everlasting covenant between God and every living creature of all flesh that is on the earth." 17 And God said to Noah, "This is the sign of the covenant which I have established between Me and all flesh that is on the earth."

Can you imagine what this rainbow looked like to Noah and his family? The most beautiful, vivid colors that they had ever seen were displayed. The warmth of knowing that God's judgment had relented filled their hearts. As with any covenant that God makes with mankind, the adversary, Satan, seeks to pervert it. At this point you may be asking the question, "What does the story of Noah have to do with this book? Even though the Lord may not intend to destroy the earth again with a natural flood, He is planning to flood the earth again. If so, how is God going to flood the earth and advertise its destruction for the second time?

Before the end of man's days on the earth, God is going to flood the earth with something even more powerful than water. This time He is going to flood the earth with the knowledge of His glory! Habakkuk the prophet wrote in Habakkuk 2:14, "For the earth will be filled with the knowledge of the glory of the Lord, As the waters cover the sea." Notice in this verse that Habakkuk doesn't say the glory of the Lord is going to cover the earth. He states that the knowledge of the glory of the Lord shall cover the earth.

What the scripture is saying is this; God is going to fill people with a working knowledge of how to cooperate with His glory in the last days. Water covers more than 70% of the earth's surface today. Putting that into a biblical perspective, imagine 70% of the earth's population saved, baptized in the Holy Ghost and filled with the unique understanding of how to cooperate and flow with the Holy Spirit. Today there are seven billion people on planet Earth. Imagine if five billion people (that's 70%) began flowing and cooperating with God in His glory. Think about it: walking, talking and radiating with the glory of God. If that were to happen in today's world, then the remaining two billion people could not escape the glorious presence of a mighty God. God's people would be much like Stephen in his day.

Acts 6:8-10: "And Stephen, full of faith and power, did great wonders and signs among the people. 9 Then there arose some from what is called the Synagogue of the Freedmen (Cyrenians, Alexandrians, and those from Cilicia and Asia), disputing with Stephen. 10 And they

7

were not able to resist the wisdom and the Spirit by which he spoke."

The passage goes on to state in verse fifteen that the council saw his face as the face of an angel. It was the glory of God in Stephen's life that would propel him into becoming a preaching machine and a martyr for Christ. But it was through Stephen's martyrdom that a young religious zealot by the name of Saul would become the great apostle Paul, who wrote two thirds of the New Testament that we now read in our Bible. I believe that a veritable flood stage of revival is coming to this blue ball that we call planet Earth.

In my recent travels in the United States and abroad, I am witnessing a hunger like I've never seen before. Pastors and church leaders are once again beginning to see the need for revival. In fact, here in Indiana we are in the beginning stages of revival hubs being formed in several churches across the State.

Over the last five years God has been forming and activating fivefold teams here in Indiana and abroad. In these regions where we are seeing the rivers rise and the flood stage appearing, there are some commonalities in the churches that are experiencing outpourings of God's glory. The pastors and leaders are so hungry for God that they are willing to do anything to see God move in their regions. We are seeing old rivalries between pastors being broken down and new apostolic relationships emerging. Once held religious structures are giving way to kingdom principles that are advancing God's agenda instead of man's agenda. The cities are breaking away from an empire mindset into a kingdom lifestyle.

In our city of Columbus, Indiana, many of the pastors are putting away their agendas and coming together on a weekly basis to pray and fellowship with one another. In Terre Haute, Indiana, I have witnessed a strong network of pastors and leaders who are working together to reach their city for Jesus Christ.

One of the overflows of outpouring in that city is the various outreaches that they do to reach people for the kingdom.

Another thing that I am seeing in these pockets of remnant revivalists, is the heavy amounts of saturated prayer going on in those regions, as the ministers are often found praying together. Even in Columbus, Indiana, in our prayer room at Northview Church, we have seen some very unusual signs and wonders appear in the midst of some of the local pastoral leadership as we've prayed together.

In the summer of 2017, a group of city ministers were gathered in the prayer room at Northview Church and suddenly the ministers began to witness what looked like oil appearing on the north wall of the prayer room. The small 180 square foot triangular shaped room was glowing with a glistening-like substance unlike anything that I've seen before. We noticed that as this oily substance appeared, it ran down the wall and over the world map that hung in the center of the room. The ministers were so flabbergasted that they stood there in shock. One of the ministers, in a moment of haste, took his hands and ran it through the oil and said I'm going to take this home and anoint my wife with it and pray for her diabetes. He did just that and about a week later he reported that her blood sugar A1C went down three points after anointing her with this mysterious oil. Though I don't have a perfect reason for this seemingly strange prayer meeting, I do believe that it is a sign, and I still wonder about it.

We have noted that in these regions there is a synergy happening among the city ministers. In the summer of 2017, teams from around the world converged on the emerald isle of Ireland to reach out and take the nation for Jesus. In the efforts that were put forth during this campaign, we saw ministers on the island coming together and worshiping with one another and working to bring outreach crusades all over the island during the two-week campaign.

Today many of those pastors and fivefold ministers are meeting together and praying on a regular basis. Revival hub centers are beginning to emerge, and God is stirring hearts as the rivers are peaking to flood stage. When it comes to God's church, nobody is bigger than the body of Christ. We together are getting ready to overflow the riverbanks as God's glory rises.

CHAPTER 2

A Rainbow in a Cloud on a Rainy Day

You never know what will happen in the river! In my book, River Rising, I describe the difference between the stereotypical understanding of revival and an outpouring of the Holy Spirit by using the analogy of the river. In that book, I outline six things which are not an outpouring: a church service, a series of meetings, a gifted personality, a location, a conference nor a special event. [1]An outpouring by definition is a "suddenly" from God. It is a sudden burst of the power of His Holy Spirit through which God can do anything at any given moment.

At our church here in Columbus, Indiana, we've seen a sudden outburst of the Holy Spirit happen in the most unusual situations. On one occasion we saw God save and fill people with the Holy Ghost at a wedding rehearsal. On another occasion at a church business meeting. Of all places, we saw God miraculously move at an elder board meeting when a young man knocked on our door and demanded his salvation.

Many times, God has moved at the most unusual points in a church service, as well as out in the marketplaces. You might be wondering why and how this happens. The key is in the expectation and activation of the Holy Spirit at any given point and place that you may be.

There is a culture in our church that expects God to do things in our midst at any given moment. In fact, we have adopted a slogan at our church that our folks have taken to; "Come on, Jesus, do stuff!" We believe that the focus is not on what Jesus has done in the past, though that is extremely important. Rather, we focus more upon what Jesus is doing in our midst right now. We believe that He is still "doing stuff" today. In Hebrews 13:8 the writer states, "Jesus Christ is the same yesterday, today and forever."

We tend to focus on what He's done in the past and can't wait until He reveals our future, but what we need to be focusing upon is the word today in that verse. The right question is, "What is Jesus doing today?" As I have often heard it said, we are waiting on a move of God, but God is waiting on a move of man. He's already made His move, now it's your turn to move on His behalf.

But what if I don't feel led to do stuff for Jesus? Feelings have nothing to do with the great commission of Christ. Take a look at the great commission in Mark 16:14-18. Nowhere in that commission does Christ say, when you feel led or when you feel good, or even when it is convenient for you. In verse 14 of that passage Jesus first rebukes his disciples for having hard hearts, then commissions them to go into all the world and minister in spite of their spiritual condition.

Israel was a rebellious house and because of their sins they were taken captive by the powerful Babylonians. In their times of affliction, God sends them a prophet by the name of Ezekiel. Ezekiel is praying and seeking God for the restoration of His people, when suddenly one day down by the river Chebar as he was minding his own business, the heavens opened up and he saw a vision of God that appeared before him. As you read Ezekiel 1:1-25 God reveals Himself to the prophet in stages and in different dimensions, but then the vision shifts into the appearance of a man.

Ezekiel 1:26-27: "And above the firmament over their heads was the likeness of a throne, in appearance like a sapphire stone; on the likeness of the throne was a likeness with the appearance of a man high above it. 27 Also from the appearance of His waist and upward I saw, as it were, the color of amber with the appearance of fire all around within it; and from the appearance of His waist and downward I saw, as it were, the appearance of fire with brightness all around."

Then Ezekiel gets a full-blown revelation of God.

Ezekiel 1:28: "Like the appearance of a rainbow in a cloud on a rainy day so was the appearance of the brightness all around it."

This was the appearance of the likeness of the glory of the Lord. The rainbow is an expression of the residual effects of the glory of the Lord. While I appreciate the covenant and the sign of the rainbow, I believe that we may be putting the emphasis on the wrong things here. Look at the end of verse 28: "This was the appearance of the likeness of the glory of the Lord." Some may settle for the legal binding covenant contract in this passage, others emphasize only the presence of God, but what God was trying to do was to show Ezekiel His fullness. God's desire was to reveal His glory to His people. God wanted to reveal this not just to His prophet, but to His people. It's really never about one person, one preacher or about one church. God's plan is to reveal His end-time glory to the entire world.

There are two things that happened to the man of God when he encountered the rainbow. First of all,

13

the prophet fell on his face before the rainbow (Ezekiel 1:28). Listen, if your rainbow is causing you to be lifted up in pride, then you've got the wrong rainbow. If your rainbow is causing you to fall into a perverse lifestyle of sin, then you've got the wrong rainbow. If your rainbow is causing you to rise up and slander or assault people, then you've got the wrong rainbow. Ezekiel's rainbow caused him to humble himself before God, not to rise up in rebellion against Him.

Ezekiel's rainbow did not encourage him to commit fornication or sodomy. No, his rainbow was pure and powerful enough to put the prophet on his face before a holy God. After the prophet fell upon his face, watch what God did, in Ezekiel 2:1-2: "And He said to me, 'Son of man, stand on your feet, and I will speak to you.' 2 Then the Spirit entered me when He spoke to me, and set me on my feet; and I heard Him who spoke to me." You see, the rainbow picked up the prophet, the prophet didn't pick up the rainbow.

Today we've got people hoisting the rainbow flag over their heads in pride, as if it were a license to sin with a get-out-of-jail-free card. Let me give you a prophetic word for this hour: We don't handle the glory of God; the glory of God handles us! We don't lift up the rainbow in pride, God's rainbow brings us down to a place of humility before Him. It was the rainbow that lifted up the prophet, the prophet didn't lift up the rainbow.

Ezekiel 2:8: "But you son of man, hear what I say to you. Do not be rebellious like that rebellious house; open your mouth and eat what I give you."

You can't fight rebellion with rebellion. The courts, the constitution and our politicians will not decide our battles, but rather the glory of God will! Open your mouth and speak out of His glory. Notice that the glory spoke from the rainbow, in Ezekiel 2:1: "And he said to me, 'Son of man, stand on your feet and I will speak to you.' Revelation 4:2-3 says, "Immediately I was in the

Spirit: and behold, a throne set in heaven, and One sat on the throne. And He who sat there was like a jasper and a sardius stone in appearance; and there was a rainbow around the throne, in appearance like an emerald." He destroyed the earth the first time with water, then put a rainbow seal of covenant above the earth. The next time the Lord will destroy the earth with fire! There is only one thing that will appease the judgment of God, and that's the blood-stained banner of Calvary.

In the book of Revelation 10:1 the apostle John writes, "I saw another mighty angel coming down from heaven, clothed with a cloud. And a rainbow was on his head, his face was like the sun, and his feet like pillars of fire." Now look closely at Revelation 9:21: "And they did not repent of their murders or their sorceries or their sexual immorality or their thefts." The LBGQT movement is literally flying the flag of judgment in the face of God! They are not raising a flag of appeasement, but rather of judgment. A rainbow occurs as a result of the interaction between sunlight, water and air. The light of God reveals sin. The water of God's word washes away our vain imaginations and the wind (air) of the breath of God brings refreshing to us as God works on us.

The Swelling Judgment Of God

I remember June 26th, 2015, well, as my wife and I were sitting on the beach while vacationing in Cocoa Beach, Florida. We were soaking up some much needed sunlight after several months of grueling ministry. There was sand between our toes, blue sky and direct sunlight over us. We Americans were coming out of a crippling recession and becoming more hopeful as the days passed. But as the sun went down that day, we returned to our rented beach house, and as I entered, I immediately pushed the button on the television remote control. It was then that I learned the news that the U.S. Supreme Court struck down all state bans on same-sex marriage, legalizing it in all fifty states, and requiring states to honor out-of-state same-sex marriage licenses. A deep sadness came over me and remained so during the rest of our short vacation.

Toward the end of the evening, the major news channels were reporting this Supreme Court debacle on a never-ending news cycle. Then, everything became crystal clear as the world focused its eyes upon the White House in Washington DC, which was now lit up in an array of rainbow colors. It was at that time that I realized the colors on the rainbow flag seemed to replace the colors of our patriotic Old Glory.

The prophet Amos used the analogy of the Nile River, which rose and fell annually as an example of God's judgment on Israel's pride.

Amos 8:7-8: "The Lord has sworn by the pride of Jacob: 'Surely I will never forget any of their works. 8 Shall the land not tremble for this, And everyone mourns who dwells in it? All of it shall swell like the River, Heave and subside Like the River of Egypt.'"

The moral is that the same river that God uses to bring blessings, He will also use to wash away the pollution of a society. When a river rises, it is so beautiful and majestic to see, but when that same river goes through a drought, the water recedes and exposes everything that's in the riverbed.

Many times, we don't realize what's in the heart of a man until he goes through a spiritual drought in his life. Just like a river, the debris gets exposed. But when we allow God's river to overflow in our lives, God takes all of that toxic garbage, lifts it up out of the riverbed of our heart and sends it downstream! Just as Noah was delivered through a flood, we must allow God to bring us to the flood stage in order to cleanse our hearts and our land.

CHAPTER 3

Dig Deep

There is no rival to real revival! Unfortunately, people have different ideas about what a revival is all about. When I mention the word revival, some will talk about extended meetings. Others will talk about their favorite guest speaker, and usually it will be an evangelist. Some people will have good memories, others not so good. Let's start off by looking at revival gone wrong. You see, the Garden of Eden was centered in the east and that's where Adam and Eve had their closest walk with God.

In Genesis 2:8 it says, "The Lord God planted a garden eastward in Eden, and there he put the man that he had formed." Watch what happened when Adam and Eve were kicked out of the Garden of Eden; Genesis 11:2 says, "And it came to pass that as they journeyed from the east, that they found a plain in the land of Shinar." The farther you get away from the center of God's will, the more independent and religious you become. Religion is man's attempt to get to God, but Jesus is God's attempt to get to man. If you're trying to get to God in any other way than through Jesus Christ, then you are building on sinking sand!

There are four things that I noted in Genesis chapter eleven, which records the building of the tower of Babel, that reveal a revival gone wrong. First of all, they exchanged the supernatural for the natural (Genesis 11:3 "...they had bricks for stone..."). God created the stones and man created bricks. Jesus is the chief cornerstone. Jesus is the stone that the builders rejected. Second, they tried to bring earth to heaven instead of heaven to earth (Genesis 11:4: "...a tower whose top is in the heavens;"). Your church steeple will not get you into heaven. Third, they desired to make a name for themselves (Genesis 11:4: "...let us make a name for ourselves..."). And fourth, they became exclusive in their worship (Genesis 11:4 "...lest we be scattered). When your church or group is the only way to get to heaven, then that is cultish. Jesus is the sure foundation, and you can build on no other and still get to heaven. Unfortunately, they were not building on the right foundation. In fact, they were building on sinking sand.

Here's what I believe: I believe that God wants to take us deeper into His presence than ever before and He wants a sustainable revival that never quits. The average length of revivals in church history only lasts, on average, for about five years. The question then becomes; How do we sustain revival? How do we turn our churches from a place of visitation to a place of habitation? In order to go higher up into the things of God, you have to dig deeper into His presence. Let's look at two things that will bring some insight to a sustained move of God. First, let's ask the question, what is the test of real revival? And then, what is the depth of the revival?

The Test of Revival

Many people gauge or test their revival by the fluidity and frequency of the gifts that are manifesting in their church. I've seen a great many churches flow in the nine spiritual gifts in 1 Corinthians 12, but never come close to seeing a spark of revival in those churches. Nor does bringing in dynamic gifted speakers guarantee a move of God.

Having great church services is no guarantee for revival, as I've seen churches get stuck in ruts of revival by having their yearly revival meeting series with great speakers and yet revival never seems to break out beyond their scheduled meeting times. If you're an evangelist, bringing in a set of sermons and preaching them in a church service, it doesn't mean that you will see results. Duncan Campbell once stated, "Revival is a God-consciousness even before a man ever speaks a word." True revival begins in the heart of a man, not the activities that surround a person.

Where are the preachers that are down on their faces seeking God in real time? I've met revivalists who know the language of revival but have never been in one for themselves. Just researching what God used to do in revivals and reading books about revivals may increase your appetite for revival, but it doesn't mean that you're having revival. I've seen some of the modern-day revival networks talking a lot about revival but at the end of the day it's a lot of talk but nothing to show.

My great friend, Graham Renouf from New Zealand, has told me on numerous occasions that the goal of the fivefold ministry in the body of Christ is not to teach from a lofty, soulish, theological position, but rather to "unpack what God is doing in the midst of the church in real time." When pastors get out of the way and allow God to flow, those with teaching gifts need to be ready to explain how this relates to scripture. This is what Paul was saying in 1 Corinthians 2:4: "And my message and my preaching were very plain. Rather than using persuasive speeches, I relied only on the power of the Holy Spirit." (NLT)

When real revival is flowing, lives are changed, souls are saved, people are healed and set free. After flowing in this outpouring over the past ten years in churches all over the world, I can tell you that there are more than good sermons and sporadic touches from God. Good teaching is not the test for revival. In Matthew 7, look at what Jesus says in verse 22, "...have we not prophesied, cast out demons and done many wonders in your name?" So, you're telling me that some people who are saved, filled with the Spirit and possess the gifts of heaven may, in fact, not go to heaven? How can this be? The answer is that they did not possess what they professed. They had the ministry of God but somewhere along the line they lost their relationship with Christ. When the relationship fails, usually disobedience sets in and can go virtually undetected in a minister's life.

Churches can lose the presence of God and still function in church life after the revival fires have burned out. Gifts, callings and anointing may take you far, but they will not sustain you in revival. Revival is sustained through relationship, and our relationship with God will require explicit obedience.

Matthew 7:24-26: 24 "Therefore whoever hears these sayings of Mine, and does them, I will liken him to a wise man who built his house on the rock: 25 and the rain descended, the floods came, and the winds blew and beat on that house; and it did not fall, for it was founded on the rock. 26 "But everyone who hears these sayings of Mine, and does not do them, will be like a foolish man who built his house on the sand..."

The Depth of Revival

Revival itself may not take you deeper, but when revival comes, it will reveal how deep you are! Now let's take a look at the depth of revival and how do you gauge its depth. Who will determine how deep a revival is in any revival throughout history? Go to Luke 6:46-49 and you will get an idea about the depth and gauge of revival. "But why do you call Me 'Lord, Lord,' and not do the things which I say? 47 Whoever comes to Me, and hears My sayings and does them, I will show you whom he is like: 48 He is like a man building a house, who dug deep and laid the foundation on the rock. And when the flood arose, the stream beat vehemently against that house, and could not shake it, for it was founded on the rock. 49 But he who heard and did nothing is like a man who built a house on the earth without a foundation, against which the stream beat vehemently; and immediately it fell. And the ruin of that house was great."

The depth of a true revival is found in the obedience of a submitted heart. It's not what you know, and it's not about who you know; it's what you do with who you know that matters most. Unfortunately, there are many in today's world who know about Jesus but yet they have no roots in their relationship with Him, and that is problematic to the core. That would be like someone having all of the benefits of their marriage, such as sex without intimacy, tax write-offs and housecleaning, but never connecting with their spouse emotionally. That's exactly how we approach God at times. We have a very utilitarian relationship with Him at times; you do for me, then I'll do for you. Grace is more than a get-out-of jail-free card. God is better than what He has to offer in His benefits package. He's more than a power working through us, He is our Father, our friend that sticks closer than a brother, and He will never leave us nor forsake us.

The Jewish people in Jesus' days thought they were righteous because of their ancestral connection to Abraham, Isaac and Jacob. Remember what the woman at the well said in John 4:12, "Are you greater than our father Jacob who gave us this well, and drank from it himself..." Let me translate that into modern terms for you. Are you greater than our pentecostal forefathers William Seymour, Jonathan Edwards, George Whitfield, William Booth, Evan

Roberts, R.W. Shambach, Alexander Dowie, Oral Roberts, Kenneth Hagan, and the list goes on and on.

Now, before you get offended because you think that I'm picking on your favorite preacher, or because you have a problem with anyone that I just mentioned, let me say up front that I love the stories behind all of these great giants in the faith, so I'm not here to debate their powerful footprints in history. What I want to do is to stir you up and help you into your own personal revival. I want to fan the flame on what God has already deposited in you. You see, you can't take someone where you have not gone yourself, regardless of your spiritual heritage. Psalm 42:7 says, "Deep calls unto deep..." We must learn to dig our own wells, and we dig those wells by remaining hungry for more of Him. We must remain open to what God is doing in the here and now and not the there and then.

The key to going deeper into the overflow of God is to dig the artesian wells that are presently right under your feet. If you want to go higher, you first have to dig deeper.

CHAPTER 4

Expansion

I saiah 54:1-3: 1 *"Sing, O barren, You who have not borne! Break forth into singing, and cry aloud, You who have not labored with child! For more are the children of the desolate Than the children of the married woman,"* says the Lord. 2 *"Enlarge the place of your tent, And let them stretch out the curtains of your dwellings; Do not spare; Lengthen your cords, And strengthen your stakes. 3 For you shall expand to the right and to the left, And your descendants will inherit the nations, And make the desolate cities inhabited."*

This passage is more about a relationship than it is a tent. The expansion spoken of in verses 2 and 3 is caused by a deepening relationship with God. You see, what you make room for, God will fill! In 2 Kings 4:10, the Shunammite woman hears about the prophet Elisha and his ministry. She builds a little room up on the roof of her house. Her greatest desire was to have a son. A year after Elisha moves into this little room, her wish is granted, and she has a baby boy. A few years later this young man dies, and Elisha raises him from the dead. Think about it. She builds one little room above her house and then she receives two miracles! It stands to reason since Elisha received a double portion of Elijah's spirit that she became a double portion benefactor of that impartation. Jesus said, "In my father's house there are many mansions. If I go away, I will prepare a place [room] for you." What God makes room for, He will fill.

With the expansion of this tent, we need to be reminded that we should never move out in ministry more than we go up in prayer. Your horizontal should parallel your vertical. You never go out in ministry more than you go up in prayer. Those two things are proportionally related! In other words, your relationship with your heavenly Father must deepen before expansion can happen. You can expand the tent, but if the inside is empty then all you have is a canvas ministry.

Remember Jesus' teaching on the strongman in Luke eleven? The religious leaders of Jesus day accused Jesus of casting out demons by the prince of demons, Satan. Jesus told them, "A house divided against itself shall not stand." Then he goes on to explain that when a demon goes out of a man it goes through dry places seeking rest but finding none. Afterward, the demons go and find seven other spirits, and examine the house to see if it is swept and put in order, but yet it still has the freedom to go back into this man's spiritual house. Why could this spirit go back into this man with even more demons? Because though the house was clean and in order it was empty and devoid of something extremely important: a relationship. You see, our spiritual house is empty and void when we are without Christ, and only He can fill our spiritual house with the right things.

This tent of ministry that we are speaking of in Isaiah 54:2-3 must be filled with something. What takes place in this tent is extremely important to the expansion of the tent itself. What needs to take place inside this tent is simply intimacy with the bridegroom. If we are the bride of Christ and He is our husband, then why hasn't our tent lengthened, or multiplication happened? The answer is not what the bride of Christ lacks, the answer is in the distance that has been created between God and His church. Religion drives a wedge in our relationship with our husband. The church does not lack the reproductive organs to multiply the kingdom of God. What the church lacks is intimacy with the bridegroom. The less time we spend with the bridegroom, the fewer are our chances of being impregnated with His will for our lives

The church today wants to spend an hour a week with God and yet wants a bigger tent. There are a lot of men stretching their mega tents out today, but inside them they are full of dead men's bones. They are whitewashed tombs called churches that are dead on the inside! A relationship with the father that is an inch deep and a mile wide will not impregnate us with His destiny. God is not looking for a long-distance lover, nor for a faraway fling with His bride.

In Revelation 2:1-7, God tells the largest church of its day, "...you have left your first love...repent and do the first works." It wasn't their love for Him that they lost, it was a revelation of God's love for them that they had lost. Though they left their first love, they still loved God. They had lost sight of God's love for them.

From time to time, my wife and I go back and visit landmarks where our love for each other began. We go back to the place we first laid eyes on each other and where we had our first kiss. We visit the first apartment we had after we were married. But we never go to those places to rekindle our romance with one another. When we go back to those landmarks, we go back to measure how much our love has grown with one another.

There are two things that Isaiah 54:2-3 tells us. Number one, God wants to enlarge, stretch, and lengthen our ministry influence. Number two, He wants to strengthen our relationship with Him so that we can grow healthily and safely into these new spheres of influence. To enlarge the church, the church needs to strengthen its relationship with the bridegroom. What keeps us from growing our ministries and becoming more influential? The answer to that question is found in Isaiah 54:4: "Do not fear, for you will not be ashamed; Neither be disgraced, for you will not be put to shame; For you will forget the shame of your youth, And will not remember the reproach of your widowhood anymore. Fear, disgrace and shame will sterilize a womb environment in a church."

Capacity

How much money is too much money in someone's life? One of the top CEOs in America has a net worth of $126.2 billion. Of the top grossing preachers in the world, their assets range from one million dollars to 470 million dollars in net worth. That, in comparison to the average American's median income, which is at $47,000, creates a huge wage gap. But to the average person in Southern Asia, you are a rich American. That's because their income averages somewhere between $2500 to $7000 per year. That's about a 700% difference in pay between the average Asian and us.

With all of this disparity in income, I asked the question again, "How much money is too much money in someone's life?" I recently heard a minister answer that question this way. I Timothy 6:17 states, "Command those who are rich in this present age not to be haughty, nor to trust in uncertain riches but in the living God, who gives us richly all things to enjoy." Again, the question is, how much money is too much money in someone's life? The answer is that it is too much when a person trusts more in their riches than they trust in God. This is why some people can handle hundreds, some thousands and others millions. It's all about our capacity to trust, not the capacity of our bank accounts. What he is talking about is the heart!

Solomon said in Proverbs 4:23, "Keep your heart with all diligence, For out of it spring the issues of life."

The expansion of our capacity is always connected to the level of His lordship in our daily walk with Him. You see, wealth is not the test for our spirituality, but neither is poverty. Just because someone abuses a truth, such as biblical prosperity, it does not give us the right to neglect that truth. In 3 John 2 the apostle states, "Beloved, I pray that you may prosper in all things and be in health, just as your soul prospers." I realize that prosperity isn't limited to money, but it doesn't exclude money either. Jesus said in Matthew 6:21, "For where your treasure is, there your heart will be also." It doesn't say, "Where your heart is there your treasure will be also." In other words, your heart will follow what you desire.

When I think of expansion, I always remember a character in the scriptures who would forever be remembered for his prayer for expansion in his life.

1 Chronicles 4:9-10: "Now Jabez was more honorable than his brothers, and his mother called his name Jabez, saying, "Because I bore him in pain." 10And Jabez called on the God of Israel saying, "Oh, that You would bless me indeed, and enlarge my territory, that Your hand would be with me, and that You would keep me from evil, that I may not cause pain!" So God granted him what he requested."

The word enlarge, in the Hebrew letters looks like this: רבה and it transliterates, 'raw-baw,' which means to multiply or make plenty. Jabez was making the verbal declaration of asking God to enlarge his territory. According to verse ten, God granted Jabez's request. Having a big mouth doesn't mean you have big faith, but big faith will cause you to open your mouth wide and speak out and declare the things from God's heart.

When I was a little boy, my mom used to take me into the department stores to buy me new clothes for the upcoming school year. Because I was a growing boy, she would invariably buy pants that were a little longer in length than needed so that I could grow into them throughout the school year. As a very insecure boy at the beginning of each school year, I would feel a bit awkward on the first day of school. But by the middle of the year, I would grow into my clothes. I believe that God is doing the same thing with those of us who are anticipating the next wave of revival. He is making our garment a little longer than we need, because He's making room for our growth. Right now, we may look a bit oversized and dumpy but eventually we are going to grow into a new level of revival.

On September 18th, 2018, our church was asked to pray about taking the former Assembly of God church in Edinburgh, Indiana, and replanting it as a PAC (Parent Affiliated Church) church in our district. The church had already closed down due to decline, so this would actually be more like a church plant than a church take-over. After much prayer and several confirmations, we agreed to take on this arduous task. The former church, known as the Assembly, was officially dead but God was not through with this small five-acre plot of ground with the 8,200 square foot of building that remained on it. A small remnant from the former Edinburgh Assembly had migrated over to our Columbus Campus after the church had closed its doors.

On the first day of inheriting this fifty-year-old quirky, dilapidated building, I walked in and felt the old wells of glory pulsating under my feet. I could hear the shouts of glory from revival days past. I knew that this was a God-thing and that we were to replant this church in Edinburgh, Indiana.

The Big Blue River and Sugar Creek join to form the Driftwood River just west of Edinburgh. Edinburgh, Indiana, was named in honor of Edinburgh, Scotland, a place to which some of my ancestral roots are traced. Edinburgh, Indiana, is home to just under five thousand residents, many of which carry my last name, Burton.

In the spring of 2021 my good friend, Pastor Steve Lance and his son in law, Andrew Hartley, were vacationing in Evansville, Indiana, and we asked them both to come up on a Sunday morning and minister to both our Columbus Campus and our fledgling Edinburgh Campus during morning services. At that time, we had staggered our services to occur at nine a.m. and eleven a.m. in order to allow me to attend both services. The overarching goal was to infuse the DNA of our healthier Columbus Campus into the new work in Edinburgh.

We had already scheduled one person to be baptized in water at our Edinburgh Campus, but we never dreamed that God would move 37 people to be baptized on that particular Sunday.

Pastor Steve Lance is noted, but not limited to his association with the baptismal tanks all across America. Steve was instrumental in helping baptize thousands in water at the famous Brownsville revival in the 1990's. In fact, if you watch videos of water baptisms of the Brownsville revival, you will see, Steve dunking many people in the Mikvah waters during that revival. It was on this particular day in a fiery hot Holy Ghost service in this little town of Edinburgh that I knew Edinburgh, Indiana, was going to be a special place of God's holy habitation as the river was reaching flood stage.

CHAPTER 5

Personal Revival

Vival

The word revival is not mentioned anywhere in the Bible. But the word revive is used in seven different places. Let me expound on three of them. There are three different types of revival found in the scripture; There is a national revival, which is mentioned in Psalm 85:6: "Will you not revive us again. That your people may rejoice in you?" Then there is a church revival which the prophet Habakkuk mentions in Habakkuk 3:2: "O Lord revive Your work in the midst of the years! In the midst of the years make it known..." And then there is personal revival spoken of in Psalm 119:25: "My soul clings to the dust; revive me according to Your word." God does some of His best work when He deals with our dirt. You see, a people cannot go any higher into national revival than churches in that nation first go corporately. Churches cannot go any higher into corporate revival than those in the church do in their personal lives first.

Dirt

When Jesus taught His disciples to pray, He said in Matthew 6:10, "Your kingdom come. Your will be done On earth as it is in heaven." Out of what was the first man, Adam, formed? According to Genesis 2:7, God formed man out of the dust of the earth. When Jesus is praying this prayer in Matthew 6:10 for His disciples, He is praying for them and not the earth itself, as we know it. So, the prayer might be better understood like this, "Your will be done "in earth" or in these earthen vessels as it is in heaven." That changes everything, because the emphasis goes from an impersonal responsibility to putting the onus on a personal accountability to God. In 2 Corinthians 4:7 Paul says, "But we have this treasure in earthen vessels, that the excellence of the power may be of God and not of us."

X Marks the Spot

Luke 19:5: "When Jesus reached the spot, he looked up and said to him, 'Zacchaeus, come down immediately. I must stay at your house today.'" (NIV).

God picks and knows the best spots for revival. Zacchaeus picked his spot, but Jesus came along and moved the spot. Has God ever moved the spot on you? Just when you think you've figured Him out, He moves. As a church, there is a spot that we have not reached yet. Like Zacchaeus, many times the Lord can't get revival to us because our head is too far up in the trees. We've got our heads up so high into revival expectations that we can't get to Him when He passes by. There is no difference linearly or vertically if there's distance between you and Him. There is no difference if there is distance in the relationship. It's not landmass, trees or the sky that separates us from Jesus. It's our understanding of Him that does so. Proximity is the measuring stick of holiness.

31

Leonard Ravenhill once said, "No man is greater than his prayer life. The pastor who is not praying is playing; the people who are not praying are straying. We have many organizers, but few agonizers; many players and payers, few pray-ers; many singers, few clingers; lots of pastors, few wrestlers; many fears, few tears; much fashion, little passion; many interferers, few intercessors; many writers, but few fighters. Failing here, we fail everywhere." The church appears to be better fed than led. Lots of teachers, not many fathers and a very quiet and subdued Holy Spirit. It's time for change.

In January 2021, Cindy and I felt compelled to connect with a revival hub that was brewing in Peoria, Arizona. After connecting with the Fresh Start church and their pastors, Paul and Kim Owens, we had a new fire lit under us and we came home with a renewed passion for prayer. Beginning in July of that same year, we took a leap of faith and changed our Wednesday night programs to a night of intercessory prayer. We were surprised as each Wednesday night our numbers began to grow as the people bought in hook, line and sinker.

I call our intercessory prayer nights the most unselfish nights of the week. During the evenings we make declarations and do as Abraham did, calling things that are not as though they were so. Since the beginning of this new prayer directive, we have seen remarkable signs, wonders, miracles and healings. We call out family members to be saved and God is honoring these declarations. On April 11th, 2022, Cindy and I led my 84-year-old dad in the sinner's prayer, and he received Jesus Christ as his Lord and savior! As Daddy prayed for God to save his soul, genuine conviction came upon him, tears filled his eyes and he cried out to God for forgiveness. Just days before, on a Wednesday night, we were making verbal declarations that our families would be saved. We called out their names and claimed their souls for Jesus. God heard our prayers and on that next

Monday my daddy met the risen savior.

A Touch Too Much

Recently, during one of our Wednesday night prayer meetings, I sat down on the stage after about three waves of glory came into the sanctuary. As I sat there with my head down, the Holy Ghost swooped into my heart and asked me the question, "Do you want a touch, or do you want to touch something?" My eyes popped open wide as I knew His distinctive voice resonated over the music and the voluminous prayer declarations being released into the atmosphere. I, being the spiritual man of God that I am, retorted back to the Holy Spirit, "Can you give me some scripture on that?" He quickly reminded me of Moses and his mountain top experience in Exodus.

The scripture says that Moses was the humblest man on the planet in his day.

Numbers 12:3: "Now the man Moses was very humble, more than all men who were on the face of the earth."

Why was Moses such a humble man? The reason that Moses was more humble than anyone else on the planet was simply that he spent more time with God than anyone else on the planet. Obviously, Moses was not stating this about himself because if he did, he would lose the title by default of being God's most humble servant. Someone once said, "Humility only grows over the grave of pride." The more time that you spend with God, the bigger He gets and the smaller you become.

When Moses went up on Mount Sinai to pray, he would go into the Tabernacle and meet personally with God, but the congregation was happy to worship God at home standing in front of their tent doors.

Exodus 33:7-11: 7 "Moses took his tent and pitched it outside the camp, far from the camp, and called it the tabernacle of meeting. And it came to pass that everyone who sought the Lord went out to the tabernacle of meeting which was outside the camp. 8 So it was, whenever Moses went out to the tabernacle, that all the people rose, and each man stood at his tent door and watched Moses until he had gone into the tabernacle. 9 And it came to pass, when Moses entered the tabernacle, that the pillar of cloud descended and stood at the door of the tabernacle, and the Lord talked with Moses. 10 All the people saw the pillar of cloud standing at the tabernacle door, and all the people rose and worshiped, each man in his tent door. 11 So the Lord spoke to Moses face to face, as a man speaks to his friend..."

The congregation was content to watch their leader get closer to God but they themselves would watch from afar. They were used to worshiping vicariously through their "pastor" instead of going up higher themselves. In a real sense they were looking for a touch, but their leader, Moses, was more interested in touching God in his own authentic experience.

I have witnessed many times as worship teams on the stage appear to be having a lot more fun than the people who are supposedly worshiping God out in the crowd. On the other hand, I've witnessed church leaders watch their congregations worship God while they stand idly by and wait for them to get done in order to preach their sermons. The stage show must stop! There is no such thing as a worship concert. Worship is worship and a concert is a performance. Entertainment church must be replaced with an encounter church! God is not on display for you and me to watch Him perform, God is alive and ready for His creation to interact with Him in a personal, intimate manner.

Today, preachers are laying hands on dead people in dead congregations, trying to impart life into people who are perfectly satisfied with being dead. The Levitical law forbade priests from touching dead bodies. Preacher, your anointing is either a transfusion of God's power into the weak or it's an embalming fluid to those who are spiritually dead. Jesus said, "Let the dead bury their dead." Don't waste the anointing!

When God moves in an outpouring, He's moving on and touching flesh (Joel 2:28-32). During the first 10 years of outpouring at our church in Columbus, Indiana, God was gloriously moving by the power of His Spirit. People were jumping into the river in His presence and receiving fresh impartations weekly. We've seen much fruit come because of these wonderful times of refreshing. A world-renowned prayer room, several evangelistic ministries and many signs and wonders have transpired because of this outpouring river at Northview Assembly of God Church. Scores of people have had genuine encounters with God that have changed their lives during the outpouring.

However, two years ago, God spoke to me during my quiet time with these words, "How long are you going to keep my people cocooned in the outpouring?" I froze in my tracks as I pondered the question. As I went on with my day, I finally asked the Lord, ``What do you mean 'cocoon your people?'" I remember Him stating emphatically, "As long as they have an outpouring mentality, they will never go up higher into the revival that I want to do in them, in you, in your territory and in the world." For me it was like a lovers quarrel in which neither of us spoke to each other for hours. Finally, I got before Him and repented and said Father, "I'll do whatever you want to do." As I said that, it was as if something broke inside me. It was as if my spirit had fallen from a high cliff in a freefall without a parachute.

Since that day, our church has gone through some of the greatest spiritual warfare since we founded the church in 1995. Conversely, since accepting God's challenge to go after revival, we have had some of the greatest breakthroughs and victories than ever before in our church's history. You see, an outpouring is about conquering the room, whereas a revival is about taking that room and conquering the city, nation and world. It's all about what your focus is. The first thing that Joel mentions after a latter-rain (outpouring) is sons and daughters being saved and prophesying. The river is rising, and the flood stage is upon us. Are you ready?

CHAPTER 6

The Secret Ingredients of Revival

You can't have the greater thing if you're not willing to do the lesser. Kentucky Fried Chicken (KFC) is now a world-renowned food franchise. The colonel began franchising the restaurant at the age of 64 and sold the successful KFC business at age 74. Today Kentucky Fried Chicken has an estimated net worth of 15 billion dollars. That's not bad for an elderly man with a passion for chicken and a vision to serve it to the world. So, what was the Colonel's secret to success? According to Sanders, the secret to great chicken was his eleven herbs and spices. And for years people have tried to figure out what those herbs and spices are and how the Colonel perfected his chicken.

I am sure that you're asking the question, what does Colonel Sanders have to do with revival? In Genesis 22:1-19, which is the story of Abraham's willingness to sacrifice his son Isaac on a make-shift altar to God. In the story you'll find at least six secret ingredients to revival. As you read, you'll see the contrast between an Isaac understanding of revival, and an Abraham understanding of true revival.

The first ingredient is found in Abraham's

ability to lead. Abraham's leadership is tested through his obedience to God.

Genesis 22:1: "Now it came to pass after these things that God tested Abraham, and said to him, 'Abraham!' And he said, 'Here I am.'"

Real leaders answer to God by saying, "Here I am," not with, "I'll be there in a minute!" The following are a couple of examples of prophets in scripture who gave the right answer when God came calling. The first is a young prophet in the making by the name of Samuel, who answers in 1 Samuel 3:4: "The Lord called Samuel. And he answered, 'Here I am!'" The second example is of an older more seasoned prophet's response found in Isaiah 6:8: "Also I heard the voice of the Lord, saying: 'Whom shall I send, And who will go for Us?' Then I said, 'Here I am! Send me.'" A profound face to face encounter with God changes the response time that we have after He assigns us a task.

On the other hand, there are examples of men who ran from the calling of God in their life after years of encounters with Him. Adam had spent years in the garden communing with God. After Adam and Eve had sinned, the Lord came looking for them in the cool of the day, in order to meet with them at their usual rendezvous, but Adam was nowhere to be found.

Jonah was a good Jewish boy, raised up right, and a true patriot to his country. Yet one day when God came calling, Jonah balked at the assignment and took a boat in the opposite direction of God's clarion call to Nineveh.

What did Adam and Jonah have in common? Both had a crystal clear calling on their lives but also a lack of trust in their relationship with their maker. Somewhere in the relationship they developed a mistrust in their assignments. John Wesley was once quoted as saying, "Give me one hundred preachers who fear nothing but sin, and desire nothing but God, and I care not a straw whether they be clergymen or laymen; such alone will shake the gates of hell and set up the kingdom of heaven on Earth."

The second ingredient is found in Abraham's determination to worship God.

Genesis 22:5: "And Abraham said to his young men, 'Stay here with the donkey; the lad and I will go yonder and worship, and we will come back to you.'"

True leaders are worshippers. You can't be a stubborn mule, sit in the same place, sing the same four songs every week and call yourself a true worshipper of God. Abraham made the statement, "You sit here, and I and the lad will go over yonder to worship." In revival, true worshippers are willing to go over yonder with God.

In Hebrew the word yonder means way over there to the other side. In other words, revival leaders should be willing to go further than the people that they are leading. Many times, in our quest to be authentic in our church services, we can miss the authenticity of our own experience with God. I've seen this time and again with Christian leaders, especially senior pastors. They are so concerned about a true move of God that they miss the point of a move of God in the first place.

A move of God isn't for God's sake; a move of God is for our sake. We need God to move on our behalf! Those in leadership who are seeking an authentic move of God usually don't put that same demand on their worship leaders, their programs, or their sermons. It appears that we are okay with regurgitated gobbledygook in all these areas of ministry. However, when it comes to a move of God we bristle and put such a demand on a move of God that it becomes impossible for God to manifest, let alone to move in a church service.

The third ingredient is Abraham's ability to carry the fire of God in his life. In verse six Abraham took the fire into his own hand and prepared to make a sacrifice. According to one source, [1]it appears that God's sacrifices, at least those requiring a burnt offering, were made with fire started by God Himself, usually by fire falling from heaven. This was also a sign that a sacrifice was accepted. The fire he carried would have kept burning since the time that God had sent fire from heaven. Jesus carried such a fire that even after His resurrection people bore witness to it. Luke 24:32: "And they said to one another, 'Did not our heart burn within us while He talked with us on the road, and while He opened the Scriptures to us?'" If you've got a fire in your belly, then others will feel the heat of your passion.

The fourth ingredient is found in Genesis 22:9: "Then they came to the place of which God had told him. And Abraham built an altar there and placed the wood in order; and he bound Isaac his son and laid him on the altar, upon the wood." Revival leaders lead the way and pay the ultimate price in sacrifices. Abraham's obedience to God and willingness to give up his only son is a picture of the nature of God's heart toward humanity. It was God himself who laid His only begotten son on the altar of sacrifice and paid the penalty for our sins.

The fifth ingredient of revival is found in the understanding of provision. Genesis 22:14:

"And Abraham called the name of the place, The-Lord-Will-Provide; as it is said to this day, 'In the Mount of the Lord it shall be provided.'"

The difference between Abraham's and Isaac's understanding of revival is found in Genesis 22:7: "But Isaac spoke to Abraham his father and said, 'My father!' And he said, 'Here I am, my son.' Then he said, 'Look, the fire and the wood, but where is the lamb for a burnt offering?'" I believe that Isaac's question is a fair one, considering he's the one being asked to lay face up on the altar as his dad's shiny knife catches his eye. But watch what happens in Genesis 22:13:

"Then Abraham lifted his eyes and looked, and there behind him was a ram caught in a thicket by its horns. So Abraham went and took the ram, and offered it up for a burnt offering instead of his son." Notice the difference between Genesis 22:7, where Isaac asks for a lamb for the altar and in Genesis 22:13 where God provides a ram in the bushes. So, what's the big deal?

The Hebrew word for lamb is the word śê, and it gives us a picture of a smaller, lesser animal, meekly grazing in the pasture. But the Hebrew word for ram is 'ayil, and it gives the picture of a much more forceful and majestic animal. The ram's horn was used for storing the anointing oil and as a symbol for authority. Let me put this into perspective for you.

You see, the lamb's blood that was shed for us as sinners is quintessential to everything that we do as Christians. Without the shedding of Christ's blood, we would still be entangled in our sins and bound for hell. We would be impotent against the sinful nature that plagues us from birth. But thanks be to God in that while we were still in our trespasses and sins, Christ died for us! So, what about the ram caught in the thicket? What does that mean to those of us who have been born again?

Once we are saved by the blood, we need the anointing and the authority of Holy Ghost to lead, guide and direct us in the powerful flood stage that's coming upon the earth. The body of Christ must shift its perspective of the next great revival from a docile little lamb to a powerful majestic ram of authority with fresh oil. What does revival cost a pastor and his church?

There is really no way to determine the exact amount of money that a revival costs, but in reality, it will cost you everything. Someone once commented to me about the move of God at our church. They stated, "I would kill for a church like yours." To which I replied, you don't have to kill for it, but you do have to die for it, because revival will cost you everything.

The sixth ingredient is tucked away in Genesis 22:18, God says to Abraham, "In your seed all the nations of the earth shall be blessed, because you have obeyed My voice." Think about it for a moment; the seeds of obedience can release bountiful blessings of revival to the world.

Wednesday, July 6th, 2022, our church gathered for our intercessory prayer time. After a time of brief teaching, my son, Eric Burton, took the microphone to activate the teaching during the prayer part of the meeting. Right before he proceeded to pray, I briefly took the microphone and informed the people that the offering that evening would go towards our Alaskan mission trip that Eric was heading up through his Groundbreaker International ministry. What most people didn't realize was that this upcoming conference was at a $7,000 shortfall and the monies needed to be raised before the weekend.

Unbeknownst to the spiritually hungry group that had gathered, Eric, my wife and I had gathered to discuss this very pressing issue the night before. At the end of our little conference, the Lord spoke to me about the three of us getting down upon our knees and asking for this provision for the needed $7,000. We each got out of our chairs, kneeled down and began calling out to God for help. Now when I say calling out for help, I don't mean that we were begging. No, we each were crying out in faith in earnest, knowing that God was going to answer.

After we finished praying and stood up to assess our prayer time, my wife enthusiastically raised her voice and said, "I can't wait to see what Jesus is going to do!"

So, during our Wednesday night prayer time, Eric grabbed the microphone and proceeds to pray for our trip to Alaska, among several other missional needs in the church. At one point during the prayer time, our elder, Curt Fish, walked up to Eric and whispered something in his ear as the music faded. Curt then took the microphone and declared a personal gift of $1,000 toward the Fire on the Ice campaign. Quickly, the Lord spoke to me about matching that $1000 and Cindy and I publicly shared our intentions of giving. Soon after that, people were walking up to the white offering buckets, located on the stage and began putting money into the coffers. Before the night was over, over $7,500 had been raised for this very strategic outreach, slightly over the needed amount due in just three days.

Paul shared his excitement with the church at Philippi after receiving a generous offering from them.

Philippians 4:19: "And my God shall supply all your need according to His riches in glory by Christ Jesus."

He wasn't speaking of himself in this verse, he was speaking of the blessings that they would receive because of their obedient generosity toward him and his ministry.

Here is the key to having an Abraham understanding of revival in Genesis 22:19: "So Abraham returned unto his young men, and they rose up and went together to Beersheba; and Abraham dwelt at Beersheba." Beer-sheba means, "well of the sevenfold oath." We must make a commitment to go back to the wells of revival and drink from them continuously.

What is a well? A well is an excavation or structure created in the ground by digging, driving, or drilling to access water. The oldest and most common kind of well is a water well, which accesses groundwater in underground aquifers.

What is an aquifer? Aquifers are bodies of saturated rock and sediment through which water moves. Aquifers provide 99% of our groundwater, which becomes our drinking water. God created these aquifers as a purification system for our drinking water. The purity of the well that you drink from is dependent upon how deep you go and the aquifers which help you filter impurities out of your life.

I have some great friends in my life who serve as aquifers for my well. These are bona-fide fivefold men of God whom I am privileged to access at any point when I am in a struggle, have a conflict or just for personal fellowship time. Keith Taylor, Fred Aguilar, Michael Livengood and Graham Renouf are a few of them. Why would I name drop on these people in particular? It's not to curry favor or to get something out of them. It's because I've spent massive amounts of time with them. I've traveled the world with these men, preached in meetings with them, stood shoulder to shoulder as we prayed for the sick, and cast out demons.

It's like a band of brothers who have gone to war together and spent time in foxholes with incoming rounds from the enemy. The stories are numerous, and the fruit and character are obvious to me. These are A-list fivefold men, that's why I can freely mention them in this book. Here is a great question for you; who are the aquifers in your well? Who are the people that help you filter your doctrinal thinking, your emotions, and your experiences?

CHAPTER 7

Apostolic Aquifers (Aqua Men)

The scripture plainly states in Ephesians 2:19-22, "Now, therefore, you are no longer strangers and foreigners, but fellow citizens with the saints and members of the household of God, 20 having been built on the foundation of the apostles and prophets, Jesus Christ Himself being the chief cornerstone, 21 in whom the whole building, being fitted together, grows into a holy temple in the Lord, 22 in whom you also are being built together for a dwelling place of God in the Spirit."

As we described in chapter six, an aquifer is God's way of purifying our groundwater, which in time becomes our drinking water. One of the keys to the end time revival is the restoration of the fivefold ministry gifts to the body of Christ. It is not that God ever dissolved the fivefold ministry, but because of abuses in the church, well-meaning men, by their own volition, caused the emphasis on these gifts to stand in a holding pattern for centuries. Just because something is abused doesn't mean that it is of no use anymore. People abuse vehicles, weapons, the internet, government, first and second amendment rights and even other people, but that shouldn't nullify the validity of these rights as human beings.

Acts 4:33-34: 33 "And with great power the apostles gave witness to the resurrection of the Lord Jesus. And great grace was upon them all. 34 Nor was there anyone among them who lacked; for all who were possessors of lands or houses sold them and brought the proceeds of the things that were sold..."

The word great is the Greek word megas, and it means big, larger, louder or more mature. Megas is where we get the word mega from. The apostles were operating in great (mega) resurrection power, and because of this, the church was flowing in the great (mega), unparalleled, unadulterated, unmatched, unprecedented, unmerited grace of God!

The early church was functioning at an optimum level because things were being set in their proper order by the aquifers, the apostles. If you look at the fruit that followed this, you'll see that the spirit of poverty was broken in this region. True apostles will always attack the poverty mindset. The word lack in verse 33 is the Greek word endeēs and it connotes someone being put into chains. When there is a spirit of poverty in a region, it keeps the people bound in the chains of misfortune.

What is the spirit of poverty? Is it based on income inequality? Or is it possibly a sinister governmental conspiracy to keep certain segments of society in check? I believe that the actual spirit of poverty is at work when Satan has blinded the eyes of people to the true blessings of God. Sometimes it is accompanied by a false sense of humility that equates being poor with God's grace.

Paul brings this to light when he writes to the church at Galatia in Galatians 6:7: "Do not be deceived, God is not mocked; for whatever a man sows, that he will also reap." Paul uses the Greek word for deceived (planaō), which means to roam (from safety, truth, or virtue), to go astray, deceive, err, seduce, wander, be out of the way. The deception of poverty comes as a result of not trusting God to come through with His end of the bargain. Even though God has set in order the universal principle of reciprocity, sowing and reaping, many people have a hard time trusting God for the return on their investment into the kingdom. Why is this true?

Have you ever purchased a pack of seeds from your local store? When you look at the packet of seeds, you'll only see a picture of the harvest that comes from those seeds and not the seeds themselves. Why? Because people identify with the harvest, and not the origin of the harvest. Therefore, the seed sellers only put pictures of the produce on the packets and not the seeds. In the same way, on far too many occasions we preachers mainly focus on the beauty of the harvest with very little mention on the time, work and patience needed to get a harvest.

Jesus even dealt with this disparity during His ministry on earth. In His own words in John 4:35-36, He says, 35 "Do you not say, 'There are still four months and then comes the harvest'? Behold, I say to you, lift your eyes and look at the fields, for they are already white for harvest! 36 And he who reaps receives wages, and gathers fruit for eternal life, that both he who sows, and he who reaps may rejoice together." In those two verses we find the key to breaking a spirit of poverty in the concept of work and trust.

When we put the work in, we can expect to get a return, or wages earned for our efforts. Paul stated in 1 Corinthians 3:6-8: "I planted, Apollos watered, but God gave the increase. 7 So then neither he who plants is anything, nor he who waters, but God who gives the increase. 8 Now he who plants, and he who waters are one, and each one will receive his own reward according to his own labor." Trusting God is the key element in breaking these cycles of poverty in our life.

The ultimate reason that poverty needs to be broken is that the kingdom of God needs to be expanded. For that reason, there needs to be apostolic government set up to break these chains from the cities that we live in. Many churches today are operating in minimal power and not in the maximal power that God has to offer. The word dunamis is one of four great power words in scripture. The others are exousia, delegated authority; ischuros, great strength (especially physical); and kratos, dominion authority. Dunamis means energy, power, might, great force, great ability, strength. The apostles were demonstrating mega dunamis that was breaking the back of poverty in their regions.

Best Foot Forward

Both Isaiah 52:7 and Romans 10:15 refer to the feet of those who are sent to preach the gospel of Christ. The word sent is the Greek word apostellō [ap-os-tel'-lo] and is where we get our word for apostle. An apostle is sent out on a mission. True apostles understand that they are in a mission for Christ and must be in submission to Him. In Ephesians 6:20, the apostle Paul referred to himself as "an ambassador in chains."

Unlike some modern-day apostles and prophets, the early apostles were not elitist rogues who operated independently from the local church with no accountability other than that of Christ Himself. Each of them had deep roots and accountability to the local church. 2 Timothy 1:1: "Paul, an apostle of Jesus Christ by the will of God, and Timothy our brother, unto the church of God which is at Corinth, with all the saints which are in all Achaia." The early apostles did not see themselves as superior to the local church, but rather as a servant of God to His people (Romans 1:1; Titus 1:1).

Jesus set this example when he stooped down and washed His disciples' feet. Between Acts chapter four and five I have found at least five references to the apostles' feet. Why are their feet important to us? Because our feet are representative of our ministry.

Remember, according to Isaiah 52 and Romans 10, our beautiful feet are carriers of the gospel. In Acts chapter 4:35-37 we find that many people who possessed land, sold their property and took the money that they had received and laid it at the apostles' feet. Why the feet? Because this was where the ministry engine of the church began, at the feet (or ministry) of the apostles.

Now Acts 4:35 gives us the reason that the apostles were entrusted with this large amount of money: "...and they [the apostles] distributed to each as anyone had need." As an example of how the office of an apostle works in regard to the distribution of kingdom money, my friend, Glenn Dunlop, from Belfast Ireland breaks it down this way: "If you give the money to a prophet, he'll have a prophetic conference. If you give it to an evangelist, he'll have a crusade. Give it to a pastor, he'll give it to families in the church. Give it to a teacher, he'll buy everybody a Bible. But give it to an apostle, he'll give some to the prophet, some to the evangelist, some to the pastor, some to the teacher and keep some to himself. This will keep everybody empowered and all the wheels of the church turning in the right direction." The scripture gives us an example in Acts 4:35: "...and laid them at the apostles' feet; and they distributed to each as anyone had need." The word distributed means to divide among others.

Now when we move on into Acts chapter five, we find something a little more sinister going on at the apostle's feet. A married couple by the name of Ananias and Sapphira had sold their property as others had previously done. Only this time they contrived together to give part of the money to the apostles and keep some of it back for themselves. This would not have been a problem, except that they were trying to make themselves look good by giving the appearance that they had given the whole amount when they kept some back for themselves. The question might come up, why was God so harsh in his judgment against these two and not others? No doubt this was not a first-time offense in withholding money from God in human history.

The reason that this extreme judgment came was the new fledgling church could not start out with this type of impurity in its DNA. Watch what happens in Acts 5:9-10: "Then Peter said to her, 'How is it that you have agreed together to test the Spirit of the Lord? Look, the feet of those who have buried your husband are at the door, and they will carry you out.' 10 Then immediately she fell down at his feet and breathed her last. And the young men came in and found her dead, and carrying her out, buried her by her husband." Notice that both Ananias and Sapphira fell down dead at the apostles' feet. Again, the feet of the apostles are symbolic of the engine room of the church, the ministry. Note that they didn't fall at the prophets' feet, at the evangelists' feet, nor the pastors' feet. No, they fell at the beautiful feet of the apostle. And because of this incident, great fear came upon the church (Acts 5:11).

Let's keep looking into Acts chapter five, as something remarkable happens there. Because of the purging of these two people from the local church, great signs and wonders break out in the region. Acts 5:12: "And through the hands of the apostles many signs and wonders were done among the people..." Notice that the signs and wonders were done through the apostles' hands and not the hands of the church. In no way does this diminish the active role of believers in laying hands on the sick and casting out demons, but we do see the emphasis here in Acts put squarely into the hands of the early apostles.

There is an unmistakable breaker anointing on these early apostles in the New Testament. In looking at these two passages of scripture in Acts 4 and 5 we would conclude that what we do at the apostle's feet largely determines what the apostle's hands can do in our midst!

Conversely, if you read on in this same passage of scripture, you'll see that when the wrong people in the church try to control the money, that it ties up the hands of the apostles and keeps them from doing what they do best, and that's to govern. Ananias and Sapphira wanted to control (Acts 5:4), and that is the epitome of a religious spirit. If you can't stay in the sheepfold, don't call yourself a fivefold minister. If you want to be in the fivefold but can't stay in the sheepfold and submit to the fivefold, there's a problem in you, not the fivefold!

When a religious spirit gets into a church, it will rise up with a false sense of indignation and will determine to tie the hands of apostolic leadership. That spirit rises up to replace the established authority in the local church. Acts 5:17-18: "Then the high priest rose up, and all those who were with him (which is the sect of the Sadducees), and they were filled with indignation, 18 and laid their hands on the apostles and put them in the common prison." It was the religious leaders of the day who laid their hands on the apostles and threw them into a common prison. I truly believe that Satan's agenda is to use religion to tie up the hands of God's modern-day apostles.

Satan uses false religious indignation to tie up the hands of the apostolic gift that God uses to break open a region for God. The way that the devil goes about it is to make the apostles common or even to cancel out their appointed office.

I find it more than ironic that after the stoning of Stephen, the martyr, that the witnesses laid down their clothes at the feet of a young man named Saul (Acts 7:58), who would later become the greatest apostle in the Bible. I have likened the New Testament apostles to Charlie Brown's scraggly little tree that he brought home for Christmas. They have one ornament, they are cut down, always the sap, put on display for the world to see and they have the propensity to catch on fire. They're not much to look at, but God gets all

51

the glory through them.

If we are going to see an end-time flood of revival, there must be a renewed emphasis upon the fivefold gifts of Christ to His church, and especially the twin gifts of the apostle and prophet (Ephesians 2:20), as they work together seamlessly. The greatest move of God has yet to happen, but I believe that we are on the cusp of it. May the God who is on the move, grace us with the proper understanding and functioning of His government in these last days. Are you ready for a great move of God?

CHAPTER 8

Meander

What is a meander? [1]Meander comes from Greek Maiandros, an old name for a winding river in Asia Minor that is now known as the Menderes. Why do rivers meander? [2]Meanders are produced when water in the stream channel erodes the sediments of an outer bend of a streambank and deposits this and other sediment on subsequent inner bends downstream. Where did the term meander come from? [3]Maiandros (Maeander) was a river-god of Karia (Caria) in Anatolia (modern Turkey). [4]At one point in ancient Greek history, local rivers were worshiped by civilizations, especially throughout Greece and its colonies. Many of their cultish statues were depicted as handsome, bare chested, bearded men who reclined with a cornucopia (horn of plenty) and water jugs. The river-gods were worshiped as protectors of the young, and youths would dedicate their uncut locks to the local river at their coming-of-age.

In the scriptures we find a young prophet by the name of Elisha who had worked with and served as a protégé to the most noted and influential prophet in Israel's history, the prophet Elijah. Elisha's first miracle came at the request of the townspeople in the city of Jericho.

2 Kings 2:19-25: 19 "Then the men of the city said to Elisha, 'Please notice, the situation of this city is pleasant, as my lord sees; but the water is bad, and the ground barren.' 20 And he said, 'Bring me a new bowl, and put salt in it.' So they brought it to him. 21 Then he went out to the source of the water, and cast in the salt there, and said, 'Thus says the Lord: "I have healed this water; from it there shall be no more death or barrenness."' 22 So the water remains healed to this day, according to the word of Elisha which he spoke."

Notice that this story begins with a conflict within this city and ends with complete healing and restoration. The city itself is beautiful, pristine and desirable to live in, except that the waters upstream were polluted and the ground itself had become barren. The word barren in Hebrew is the word šākōl and implies child-barrenness. This reminds me of many churches today. They have beautiful edifices that give the appearance of health and vitality, but underneath the infrastructure the river is polluted and fruitless. I recently read a church sign that stated, "Wounded people welcome here." That certainly is a true statement, but the problem comes when the church sees itself as weak and impotent as the world around them. You see, it's one thing to identify with wounded people, but it's another thing to be identified as wounded people.

Wounded people can identify with wounded people, but wounded people cannot heal wounded people. Churches today are determined to relate to the culture around them, so much so that they are willing to change their scriptural standard. We don't intentionally become wounded to reach the wounded, nor do we intend to stay wounded to simply identify with the world around us. We are not coming from a position of weakness, but rather of victory in Christ.

We've been forgiven of the penalty of sin, but we haven't dealt with the power of sin in our lives. It is imperative to know who we are in Christ Jesus and to know who Christ Jesus is in us! Jesus said, "They that are whole need not a physician."

When you look at a mighty river flowing through the land, you rarely think about the water itself or the riverbed which the river flows through. But if you could test that water and dry that riverbed up long enough to investigate, you might be surprised at the impurities that exist.

During the first two years of the Coronavirus pandemic, the hearts of many churches and their leaders were revealed. I was surprised at the many churches that were quick to shut the doors and keep the tent folded, even after the pandemic had subsided into its second and third wave. Even more surprising is the fact that many of God's people have never returned to church since the masks came off.

The fact of the matter is that Covid revealed the hearts of many Christians and their inability to stay the course of their faith during times of trouble. What should have been a time of serious introspection in the body of Christ for some became an excuse to give up on seeking God for a spiritual flood of revival. Thank God that there have been pockets of remnant revivalists who have consecrated themselves and made the necessary corrections needed that could usher in the next great awakening.

When you look up the definition of the word meander, it not only gives you the picture of a winding river, but also of someone who wanders around without purpose. In the little New Testament book of Jude, the writer, likely the brother James, the Lord's half-brother and the leader of the Jerusalem Church, gives us some insight into this wandering vagabond spirit.

Jude 1:12-13: 12 "These are spots in your love feasts, while they feast with you without fear, serving only themselves. They are clouds without water, carried about by the winds; late autumn trees without fruit, twice dead, pulled up by the roots; 13 raging waves of the sea, foaming up their own shame; wandering stars for whom is reserved the blackness of darkness forever."

As a shepherd for over 28 years, I have seen these types of people roam into our church time and again only to leave at first offense. Some of them have come in like clockwork every time the river gets up to flood stage. Here they would come in and announce to us, "I'm back home!" Eventually, when a little conflict came up or if they didn't get their way, they would quickly disappear again without an explanation. The one thing that they have in common is a lack of repentance on their part. It's as if they are oblivious to their prior actions, coming back to church as if they are the more mature one, giving an entire church one more chance to get it right with them. They are as Jude states here, "wandering stars." My cheeky interpretation of this verse is that these types of people are wandering around looking for stardom and can't seem to find it in any church that they attend. They want to be the star of the show and want everyone doting on them and their every whim.

So, is Jude just another insecure pastor who desires to make the church all about himself? Is he a wolf in sheep's clothing who wants to manipulate his congregation? Let me help you with the answer: NO. Jude is neither insecure nor is he a manipulator. Jude goes on to give a clear understanding of how to clean out the impurities in the local church.

Look at Jude 1:19-20: 19 "These are sensual persons, who cause divisions, not having the Spirit. 20 But you, beloved, building yourselves up on your most holy faith, praying in the Holy Spirit..." As a pastor, if you are flowing in the Holy Ghost, you can tell the difference between the sensual and the spiritual when they come into your church. Make no mistake, people come into churches for various reasons. Some are moving into a new city, others are hurt and offended by their last church, some are seeking out healthy relationships in which to bring healing or security into their lives. I'm going to say this very bluntly; not many people come to a church because they are hungry for revival. They want a distinct God with a distant relationship to Him. They identify with the name on the door, the denomination in the bylaws and even parts of the local church's vision, but they only want to go so far in their relationship with God.

Jude differentiates between those who are sensual, who do not have the Holy Spirit, and those who build themselves up and pray in the Holy Spirit. Praying in the Holy Ghost is praying in tongues. But be careful not to think that just because someone once had an encounter with God and has spoken in tongues, that they are functioning in revival. The key words that Jude uses in verse 20 are "building yourselves up," which is an indication that they are remaining in the river of His presence as fruit is being produced.

The word sensual in the Greek carries the meaning of breath. Every living being whether human or animal has breath in it, but do they have the breath of God in them? Is there hunger in them for a passionate relationship with God? 1 Corinthians 2:14: "But the natural man does not receive the things of the Spirit of God, for they are foolishness to him; nor can he know them, because they are spiritually discerned."

The body of Christ has to take care of these issues of pollution before Christ's second coming. Just as Elisha did, we must go to the source of the polluted water and throw in the salt. Remember that Jesus referred to his church as salt and light to the world around them. According to evangelist Perry Stone, [5]to this day, there is a freshwater spring at Jericho identified as the "Springs of Elisha," that has served as the town's fresh water source for centuries.

CHAPTER 9

"Flamous"

The Egyptians worshiped it, the Pharaoh's resourced it, and as an infant, Moses survived it. We are talking about the most famous river in the world, the Nile River. The Nile runs 4,132 miles in length. [1]Rivers are the lifeblood of our world. Providing water supplies to ecosystems across the globe, these natural flowing watercourses provide habitats, energy, transportation and sources of recreation. Usually, the size and length of a river determines its fame. The ancient Pharaoh's tax collectors determined the farmers dues based upon the inundation of the Nile River. In other words, the deeper the Nile would get, the more money a farmer would have to pay into the Egyptian tax system. Likewise, as we go deeper into the river of God's presence, the more it will cost us.

They will judge it by how many years that it ran, by how many souls were projected to have been saved, and so on. If we are not careful, the revivalists of today can become the Pharisees of the next revival. These are sincere people who are fighting against its flow as ignoble crusaders who believe that they are in God's will. I have heard it put this way; when the outgoing tide of the ocean meets the incoming tide it makes that crashing sound that we hear with our ears. Much like in a move of God, the outgoing tide of revival is crashing against the incoming tide of revival, and it makes that familiar sound in our spiritual ears.

I have heard well-intentioned revival seekers say something like this, "Revival isn't about us, it's about God." While that sounds good on the surface, in reality it is only partially true. I understand that our focus in obtaining revival must be upon God, but ultimately revival is about people, cities and regions being transformed into His image. C. S. Lewis once said, "Humility is not thinking less of yourself, it is thinking of yourself less." You see, God doesn't need revival, but we do.

The sea of Galilee is actually a lake which is fed by a river. Galilee is where Jesus began His earthly ministry.

Matthew 4:23-25: 23 "And Jesus went about all Galilee, teaching in their synagogues, preaching the gospel of the kingdom, and healing all kinds of sickness and all kinds of disease among the people. 24 Then His fame went throughout all Syria; and they brought to Him all sick people who were afflicted with various diseases and torments, and those who were demon-possessed, epileptics, and paralytics; and He healed them. 25 Great multitudes followed Him--from Galilee, and from Decapolis, Jerusalem, Judea, and beyond the Jordan."

One of the greatest challenges of any revival is the fame that comes with it. When Jesus began His earthly ministry, He started it after a prolonged fast of forty days and forty nights in a wilderness/desert experience. Remember that the same Spirit that lit upon Jesus at His baptism is also the Spirit that led Him into the wilderness to be tested. Soon after His test in the wilderness He begins to lay hands on the sick and to deliver those who were held captive by the devil. When God starts moving and the signs and wonders start compounding, it becomes impossible to keep it a secret anymore. Jesus immediately became famous and because of his fame He also amassed a huge following of people. Fame and a following are incredibly heavy burdens to deal with. I have watched people develop a following in order to get famous, but Jesus did the opposite. He gathered the following (disciples), and in time, He became famous.

In February of 1964, the Beatles were international stars and had achieved unprecedented levels of critical and commercial success. We are all familiar with the boys from Liverpool, England, and their skyrocketed rise to fame. Though they enjoyed their magnanimous success to the top, it would eventually become obvious that this kind of stardom came with all the trappings that we've seen played out over and again with rock stars and movie stars. Fame can create a bubble that insulates the famous from the flame that's needed to keep them grounded.

I once watched a young man use his charisma and his social media page to get a following of people. He would post against other ministers and raise all kinds of controversial subjects just to draw people to his Facebook page. As he continued to chisel away at the credibility of the local churches and their ministers, he began to introduce his newly acquired following to the grandiose ideas of his imaginary church. He would tout to his audience his views, values and eventual vision of what could be possible if he were in charge. Soon afterward he was successful in getting a few religious leaders to give him a fivefold ministry title. As his untested "ministry" gained a following, he made the grand announcement to his followers, "I am starting a church." Of course, everyone who followed him online needed no convincing because they had firsthand evidence of his ministry credibility. After all, he had preached a few sermons, had counseled a few people and even led a few to Christ along the way, so why would anyone question his readiness for the pastoral ministry. His voice was strong on Facebook, with opinions, theories and gaslighting, but he built his fame without a flame. He had managed to convince people that his ministry was the answer to the ineptitude of the other fivefold ministers in his city, therefore qualifying himself as the new sheriff on the block. Unfortunately, he found out over time that leading actual people was a lot more challenging than pastoring the virtual church. In the wake of his shortcomings and failures, many lives were ruined by his inability to walk things out with his new parishioners.

I recently received an apology through instant messenger from a young evangelist who had ministered at our church at one of our outpouring services many years before. When he initially came our way and dropped anchor, he was full of life, hope and idealism. He was new in the ministry, and we recognized the calling and gift-mixes, so we scheduled him in for a meeting. It became apparent very quickly that he thought that he had the world by the tail as he boasted of all his ministry experiences.

After the evening service, we had a meal together with him and he shared with us about all of his experiences. Unfortunately, they were not experiences that he had gone through, but rather places that he wanted to go, and things that he desired to see happen in his ministry. Too many "wanna-be preachers" today are theorists and not practitioners when it comes to serving God. They know things, yet they've done few things in actual ministry.

The religious people of Jesus day thought that they knew more than Christ himself. They thought that their knowledge of God would somehow get them closer to God. Some people think that they know more than I do, and I am fine with the logic of that, but if you know more than I do, then you had better be doing more than I do, because you're going to be accountable, not for the more that you know, but for the less that you are doing.

The following is a whimsical but surreal

description of a modern day pastor: "[2]If a pastor preaches over 12 minutes, he's a windbag; if his sermon is short, he came unprepared; if he gives his sermon in a quiet voice, he's a bore; If he puts feeling into a sermon, he's too emotional; If the church budget is balanced, he's a good businessman; if he asks for money to balance the budget, he's greedy. If he visits church members in their homes, he's nosy; if he doesn't, he's a snob and doesn't care. If he's young, he's not experienced enough; if he's old, he should retire. If he lives, the pastor at the church down the street is a better preacher and counselor than he is; if he dies, there was nobody like him, and his equal will never be seen again."

God is not interested in making you famous, His intention is to make you "flamous!" He wants to set you on fire with His glory and to watch you burn for Him. Throughout history, in every great move of God, there is someone that historians will point to as catalyst in that revival. They are men and women that God used in powerful ways to channel a great awakening to enact cultural transformation. Revivalists John Wesley, Duncan Campbell and Evan Roberts each brought refreshing new challenges to their world, which in turn became a tidal wave of God's glory to overpower sin-sick societies.

Here is a thought-provoking question; what if the history of the next revival is written by the people who missed out on the rapture of the church? If it were to happen that way, their report wouldn't be about the famous preacher that God used to spearhead this great revival. It will be all about Jesus who came down in the twinkling of an eye and snatched away all of those Christians from this perilous world. Many people are going to be surprised after they get to heaven and learn how differently God sees revival than we do.

God's greatest desire is for His creation to be with Him eternally. God may not be as focused on the revival leaders themselves as He is on the people who were obedient to Him to bring souls into the kingdom of God. What about the massive prayer efforts that went into the revivals that we champion? What about the scores of little old ladies who darkened their prayer closets, only to turn on the light of God in their city? The story may be written differently in heaven. Regardless, you see, God gets the glory, and we get the story.

CHAPTER 10

Flow

Most ministries today have a singular leader when it comes to service flow in the local church or during special church related events. And while it is important to have a point leader, it is extremely important for that leader to know the gifts and talents of those gathered around them. As times of revival begin to expand, it is imperative for the church to flow properly for the greatest impact. Some have marveled at the team approach which my fivefold ministry friends demonstrate as we flow together during ministry gatherings.

Many services, both at home and overseas, have demonstrated unselfish submission as we move with God in real-time. More than just sharing a microphone or being the master of ceremonies for an event, we have learned to flow with what God is doing in the moment. At times we are in a holy huddle to determine the direction of a service, and at other times it's simply to determine which gift or office will fit into one particular spot in a conference. Regardless of who, what, or when, we as a team recognize our own gifts as well as those that we work with in order to accomplish the task at hand.

Early on in the infant stages of the outpouring which began twelve years ago in Terre Haute, Indiana, at Cross Tabernacle Church, God began to put the pieces of a relational puzzle together which has made an impact that has lasted until today. These relationships with a fivefold team concept have been extremely effective, especially when we work together. I have remarked to others that when I go out to minister alone, I feel naked without my teammates. It's not that I don't have a gift or something to offer to a church, but after flowing with a team, it can be very limiting.

If you search the scriptures thoroughly, you'll soon come to the realization that both Jesus Christ and the apostle Paul of Tarsus operated and flowed in team ministry. Why is team ministry so important? Because, unlike Jesus, we as individuals have limited abilities and gifts to offer when it comes to the ministry. I would sum it up like this; the team ministry approach keeps you accountable and it multiplies the resources that you need for effective ministry.

Here's a thought; if you took your car to a mechanic to overhaul your engine and he only had one tool hanging on the wall, you might lose trust in his ability to fix your car. You see, a well-trained mechanic needs many tools to get the job done. God has arranged the kingdom that way too, He has many tools that he uses in order to get the job done and to ultimately get the glory from them.

When it comes to doing ministry right, it is extremely important to connect with the right people. Paul said in Ephesians 4:16, "...from whom the whole body, joined and knit together by what every joint supplies, according to the effective working by which every part does its share, causes growth of the body for the edifying of itself in love." You see you've got to be joined together before you can knit together in ministry.

The Pentagon of the Spirit

In Washington, D.C., the Pentagon is the recognizable five-sided headquarters building of the United States Department of Defense. It was built during WWII under President Franklin Delano Roosevelt's administration. It is our military planning hub that predicts and plans for military battle. 'It's the world's largest low-rise office building. It has 6,500,000 square feet of office space (three times the floor space of the Empire State Building!), 7,754 windows and 17 1/2 miles of corridors. Yet, its spoke-and-ring design means it takes only about 7 minutes to walk between the furthest two points in the building. Just as the pentagon in Washington, D.C., we need a pentagon of the Spirit in which the church's generals can come together and discuss war strategies and kingdom advancement.

As we are heading into the last days before the soon return of our Lord and savior Jesus Christ, it will be imperative that the church begins to think more militarily in its approach to kingdom strategy. We must move from a reactionary, defensive position to a more proactive, preemptive approach to the last days' battles that lie ahead. With that in mind, the fivefold ministry must get its act together and start functioning as it was designed.

We must act as generals training up the army to fight as God's warriors. We don't have time to wait for the enemy's next attack and then react in a defensive position. We must be proactive, not reactive. In the book The Art of War by Sun Tzu, he stated, "Victorious warriors win first and then go to war, while defeated warriors go to war first and then seek to win." We must understand that the battle belongs to the Lord, and we are put on this earth to enforce the victory that has already been won through Christ.

The biggest battle that we face today is not on the battlefield with our enemy, but rather within the camp of the Lord. Our spiritual generals remain isolated and out of touch with one another, which keeps them in a bubble and out of touch with the realities of their battlefield and the resources needed in order to win the war. It's high time that God's generals gather for the end-time strategy. We must learn to acknowledge one another and work together as military leaders do before we go into battle.

During his time in office, President Lincoln was notorious for spending time with his troops, especially at the hospitals where the wounded in battle were placed. He toured the Navy yards and inspected new weaponry as it came in. He visited government officials and members of congress in order to stay current on new events. He even visited battlefields, where on one occasion, he came under fire. As a leader, Abraham Lincoln kept his pulse on the nation as it was going through its most pressing time in history.

It was on October 24, 1861, that Lincoln relieved General John C. Fremont from his duties as commander of the department of the West. Fremont had become a rogue leader, bent on doing things his way. Lincoln replaced him with General David Hunter, who overtook active duties from his derelict predecessor. In a letter written shortly before Lincoln relieved Fremont from his duties he stated, [2]"He [General Fremont] is losing the confidence of men near him, whose support any man in his position must have to be successful," said Lincoln. "His cardinal mistake is that he isolates himself and allows nobody to see him; and by which he does not know what is going on in the very matter he is dealing with."

What a scathing rebuke to a once proud general whose time for inept leadership had come to an end. As I am writing this book, there have been many church leaders, generals if you will, from all walks of life, who have squandered their gifts and callings and have been relieved of their posts as kingdom commanders. Once pious generals sat at the helm of huge mega churches leading thousands into battle, only to discover their own ineptness in personal character as they were erased off the scene. Churches whose secret sins have been exposed have had their candlesticks removed from the forefront of kingdom life.

In John chapter 20 Jesus appeared to his disciples after His resurrection. As they stood in disbelief that Jesus was whom He appeared to be, He revealed to them His scars on His hands and side. In these last days, the code to open the floodgates of revival will be in our scars not in our stars! Revelation 19 outlines a time period in the future that marks the appearance of Christ in the clouds riding a white horse and with the angel armies clothed in white following Him.

But here's the problem that I see today; how are you going to ride with Him in the heavens if you can't even follow Him on the earth? You want to be in the fivefold ministry, but you won't even stay in the sheepfold. Friends, we are in a time when the river of God's presence is coming on the earth like a flood. You will either be caught up in the rising tide of His glory, or you will be washed away in the flow of His raging waters.

I recently heard some ministers discussing the difference between their churches and how they operate, as opposed to those of us who flow in the outpouring. They stated that God is doing so many new and diverse things on the earth today and that we don't have to settle on just one approach to seeking God's presence. As they debated, they made it seem that there is an option between being Holy Spirit led and other more noble ways that God is moving. The problem with their perception of how God was going to do these new things was never really explained to me in a way that made sense. It sounded like a lot of corporate terminology and lofty theory but without real substance.

Listen friends, God will never violate His word. The greater works that Jesus spoke of in John 14:12 were not different works, rather just more of the same works. In other words, we will see more healings, more

deliverance, more signs and more wonders as we
follow Him in these last days.

CHAPTER 11

Global Warming

What is it going to take to see this end-time revival upon the earth? What will move the heart and ultimately the hands of God to see this great flood stage happen? Where is the engine room that runs this massive move of God? What if I told you that the answer to these questions is simple? The answer is prayer, and furthermore, it's going to take place through the church. Jesus didn't say, "My house will be called a house of programs, or of worship, or religious duties." No, He said in Matthew 21:13, "My house will be called a house of prayer." I have researched every major revival in the history of the planet, and what I have found is that each unique revival had one thing in common; prayer preceded God's movement.

The great awakenings of the 1700s-1800s had at least three, and some have included a fourth wave of God's glory that came to the earth. Thousands of sinners were converted, countless believers were revived, many new churches were founded, the poor and the suffering were ministered to, and four colleges were birthed. All of these tremendous outpourings of God's Holy Spirit had the same undercurrent of prayer woven into them. These prayer gatherings shut down businesses and made the front pages of local and national newspapers. Though names like Edwards, Finney, Lanphier and Brainard dominate the historical landscapes of revival, it was prayer meetings led by untrained laymen that caused firestorms of God's glory that raced across the United States and touched parts of Canada. Ultimately, these floods of revival sent missionaries around the world.

In the great revival of 1830, it was reported that one hundred thousand people were reported as having connected themselves with churches as a result of that great revival. Charles Finney noted that a spirit of prayer prevailed in this revival before it ever transpired.

As the first great awakening in America waned a bit in the 1840s, only to come back in other waves, in other parts of the world God was hearing the cries for revival, and a new fire began to spread in Northern Ireland, to the likes of which Patrick would have raised an eyebrow.

In 1857 James McQuilkin, feeling the Holy Ghost to gather a few friends together for prayer, [1]took an old schoolhouse near Kells (Ballymena) where they could meet for prayer and seek God's blessing upon the work of the Sabbath School which they had recently established. Those prayer meetings caught fire in the nearby villages and then spread all over Ireland, Scotland and Wales. I have personally visited this site in Kells and you can still sense the river of God's glory running through that region.

Even in more modern-day revivals such as in Toronto, Smithton and Brownsville, the recurring theme is that prayer runs central to those revivals. What type of prayer focus will be needed for the next, and possibly the greatest move of God, ever? Even Though it may start innocently and spontaneously by unknown people, it may take some governmental help to navigate it. Because of its massive sweeping nature, more will be required of fivefold leaders to help keep the river from getting blocked. The prayer emphasis will need to shift from pastoral, local parochial parish mentality to that of apostolic planners. In his book ²Seven Power Principles That I Didn't Learn in Seminary, C. Peter Wagner notes the difference in prayer between traditional churches and apostolic churches. The following is a summary:

- In traditional churches prayer is incidental, while in apostolic churches it is central.
- In traditional churches' prayer is routine, while in apostolic churches it is spontaneous.
- In traditional churches, prayer is occasional, while in apostolic churches it is frequent.
- In traditional churches, prayer is passive, while in apostolic churches, it is aggressive. Answers to prayer are expected, they are not surprises.
- In traditional churches, prayer is quiet, while in apostolic churches it is loud. During prayer there is much more vocal audience participation, and the noise level is notable. At all times, the entire congregation will engage in "concert prayer" when everyone is praying out loud at the same time.
- In traditional churches, prayer is reverent, while in apostolic churches it is expressive. People pray with their eyes open at times, they kneel, they fall on the floor, they lift their arms up and down, and they walk around.
- In traditional churches, prayer is cerebral, while in apostolic churches it is emotional. There is much more passion in apostolic praying.

Is it possible that the end-time revival that we are speaking of today will be so sweeping, so massive and world shaking, that the body of Christ will be forced to work together?

Imagine churches swept up into this glorious river of His presence, as plans are laid aside for the King of glory to come in. What if sermons and weekly song lists took a backseat to God's agenda? Such a move of God would shift the leadership of local churches into a more functional role, and cause pastors to have to work with apostles and prophets in order to keep up with God's river. When a river is moving swiftly over its banks, you don't just swim it, you try to survive it! I do believe in global warming, but not in the ways scientists are explaining it today.

As prayer rooms are put back into local churches and God's people are compelled to steal away to their prayer closets to meet with their creator, the heat will be turned up. Eventually, the effectual fervent (red-hot boiling over) prayers that the apostle James spoke about in James 5:16 are going to melt the polar ice caps of a man-made religion.

CHAPTER 12

Drenched

According to several sources that we've obtained, there was a word given about the last days revival by Smith Wigglesworth which was given to Lester Sumrall in 1939. As WWII was ready to begin, with tears rolling down his face, Smith Wigglesworth laid his hands on Lester to pray before his departure back to America. Smith cried as he was saying, "I probably won't see you again now. My job is almost finished." As he continued to pray, he cried, "I see it, I see it!" Brother Sumrall asked, "What do you see, what do you see?" "I see the last day revival that's going to usher in the precious fruit of the earth. It will be the greatest revival this world has ever seen! It's going to be a wave of the gifts of the Spirit. The ministry gifts will be flowing on this planet earth. I see hospitals being emptied out, and they will bring the sick to churches where they allow the Holy Ghost to move."

It has also been chronicled that William Seymour, the leader of the Azusa Street revival, also prophesied that [2]in 100 years there would be an outpouring of God's Spirit and His shekinah glory that would be greater and more far reaching than what was experienced at Azusa Street. We are currently at that 100-year watermark. You can feel the rising tide of the river flowing in pockets of remnant revivalists who are putting prayer at the forefront of their religious agendas. God is obligated to hear us when we humble ourselves and turn from our wicked ways. He must answer the cries of His devoted servants who are calling on Him for personal transformation. James said, "...you have not because you do not ask. You ask and do not receive, because you ask amiss". We want transformation.

Jesus takes three of His sons in the faith with Him on a six-day journey of over 9000 feet up a mountain. Peter, James and John were getting ready to go on an accelerated fast track of learning with their rabbi. The scripture in Luke 19:28 states that the Lord called these three disciples up to this mountain to pray. Sounds simple, doesn't it? As they reach the peak of this mountain, Jesus begins praying, and as He prays His face changes, and His clothes begin to glisten. Suddenly, Moses and Elijah make a grand appearance and the three of them talk about His future sacrifice in Jerusalem, all while the three disciples sleep. As Peter and the other two disciples open their eyes, they are amazed at the two guests and the conversation that is taking place. Peter immediately wants to plant three churches in honor of Jesus, Moses and Elijah. But as the words roll off of Peter's tongue, a brilliant, bright cloud comes down and engulfs the entire party. In that moment all of them hear the Father's voice as He declares, this is My beloved Son, hear Him. The cloud lifts, and Jesus is the only one left standing with the three disciples.

The important thing to note is what happens in Matthew 17:2 as Jesus was transfigured before them.

The word transfigured is the Greek word metamorphoo (me-tä-mor-fo'-o), and it means to transform (literally or figuratively, "metamorphose"); change, transfigure, transform. Transfiguration and transformation have the same meaning. Isn't it interesting that today's WOKE culture throws that root word "trans" around like a one-year-old girl's ragdoll. It seems that the world wants change (trans) by going around God's plan for humanity and by altering genetics, language and culture.

As Christ and His disciples descend down that winding mountain trail, the effects of this transformational experience become evident. As they enter back into civilization, they encounter what I call the 3-D test. The first 3-D test is demons. In our passage, Jesus and the three disciples meet up with the other nine disciples as they were attempting to cast a demon out of a little boy. As they were unsuccessful in the exorcism, the post-transformed Christ rebukes them for their unbelief, their lack of faith and quickly casts the demon out of this young boy.

The second 3-D test is doubt. The disciples can't summon the faith to cast out a demon-possessed boy. This new wave of revival that we are about to enter is going to require great faith to walk it out. With these great currents in the river, we must be well read and well fed.

The third 3-D test is division. Not long after they come down the Mount of Transfiguration the disciples begin a secret conversation about who is the greatest disciple among them. Jesus catches wind of this discussion and puts an immediate end to the debate by giving them an illustrated sermon. He puts a child in their midst and tells them that the greatest will become like a child and learn to serve.

Many of God's people today are more inclined to pick up a microphone than a mop. Jesus said in John 20:16, "So the last will be first, and the first last. For many are called, but few chosen." The only way to pass the 3-D tests is by applying another D to the trial, and that is by being completely drenched in the presence of God. We understand the idea of ministering to God in worship, but do we really understand how to drink in the presence of God?

In Defense of Drinking

The 120 remaining disciples in the upper room understood the significance of drinking in the presence of God. Even though we understand Acts chapter two as the inauguration of the church, and the coronation of the disciples, there is more to the story. I love Simon Peter's explanation to the religious window shoppers as the pentecostal experience was happening in Jerusalem.

In Acts 2:14-15 it says, "But Peter, standing up with the eleven, raised his voice and said to them, 'Men of Judea and all who dwell in Jerusalem, let this be known to you, and heed my words. For these are not drunk, as you suppose, since it is only the third hour of the day.'" He uses the word "drunk" to help explain what seemed to be pandemonium to the intrigued onlookers.

The Greek word is methyō, and it means to get drunk, to be intoxicated. Metaphorically, it means one who has shed blood or murdered profusely. While that sounds a bit strange to some, it makes perfect sense to people of the Spirit. My interpretation would be that these 120 men and those in the upper room were under such spiritual duress that they lay on the floor and looked like dead men and women. I am not trying to be offensive here, but simply put into worldly terms, they were hammered, drunk, toasted, out of it, staggering drunk in the Spirit!

In the book of Proverbs 11:25 Solomon stated, "The generous soul will be made rich, And he who waters will also be watered himself." The Hebrew word for waters is the word rāvâ and it means to slake the thirst; bathe, make drunk, (take the) fill, satiate, (abundantly) satisfy, soak, water (abundantly). Now interestingly, the word for watered in this verse is a different Hebrew word. It is the word yārâ and it means to flow as water (i.e. to rain); transitively, to lay or throw (especially an arrow, i.e. to shoot); figuratively, to point out (as if by aiming the finger), to teach:—(+) archer, cast, direct, inform, instruct, lay, shew, shoot, teach (-er,-ing), through. Let me help you with this translation, we need to be teaching the people of God how to drink of His Spirit.

We must teach the younger generation how to properly drink in a culture that is obsessed with drinking alcohol as a substitute for a dry church.

Religion has declared a spiritual prohibition on the church when it comes to drinking from the wells of salvation. If you take a look at the social media pages of photos of your family and friends, you'll see many of them out on the town, taking a holiday at the beach or other types of recreation. Invariably, you will see them holding up a beer can, or wine cooler to indicate that they are having a good time. While I find it juvenile and immature to see grown men and women acting like it is some sort of rite of passage for them to drink alcohol, what they are doing is letting you know that they are a part of the culture of alcohol.

Solomon reveals the difference between spiritual drinking and natural drinking in Proverbs 20:1: "Wine is a mocker, strong drink is raging: and whosoever is deceived thereby is not wise." The question that I have for you is this; what does natural wine mock and why is strong drink raging? Wine and strong drinks are a mockery of the Holy Spirit. The apostle Paul said in Ephesians 5:18, "And do not be drunk with wine, in which is dissipation; but be filled with the Spirit."

Everyone seems to have that one uncle or even their own father who gave them their first beer. It was like being inaugurated into the club. But what if we taught our sons and daughters how to drink in the Spirit? Give them a taste of the good stuff, so that when they are presented with the wrong stuff, they will know the difference. The body of Christ is doing way too much thinking and not enough drinking.

I am loving what God is doing at Fresh Start Church in Peoria, Arizona. I am thrilled to see young men like Sean Feucht taking revival fires around the globe. It is so encouraging to hear that God is using Mario Murillo under the tents in California. The baptismal waters of Todd Smith in North Georgia are an incredible testimony to what God is doing today. And these are only a few American ministries to note.

There are a lot of higher profile people that God is using to spread revival around the world, but there are many unseen men and women that He is using to raise the river in these last days.

Here in the Midwest the I's have it. We are seeing the river surge in pockets of revival in Indiana, Illinois and Iowa. The smaller, lesser-known people and places that I am connected to are huge to the people that are being refreshed by them. I believe that we are getting ready to see these rivers go over their banks and these revivals connect the remnant to this last great end-time move of God. We are at the beginning of flood stage. Are you ready for revival?

EPILOGUE

As we come to the end of this book, I felt compelled to share with you the names of some vital ministers and their ministries that are making big impacts around the world. These are A-list revivalists that are shaking the world. If you are hungry and thirsty for more of God in your life and in your church, the following are some premiere people who can help you navigate the rising river that lies before you.

Fred Aguilar of Fire on the Altar Ministries
pastorfredaguilar@gmail.com

Eric Burton of Groundbreaker International
www.gbreaker.org

Rodney Burton of Rodney Burton Ministries
www.rodneyburton.net

James Cowan of Jeremiah 1:10 Ministries
www.j110ministries@gmail.com

Tyler Duff
www.tyler@tkdministries.com

Matthew Eckhart of Kingdom Pursuit Ministries
www.meckart1@att.net

Jordan and Kacy Cunnington of Redemption Project Ministries
www.redemptionprojectinc.org

Michael and Linda Livengood of Doorkeepers International Ministries
www.mikliven@aol.com

Nathan and Lydia Marrow of Vanguard Ministries
lydia@vanguardministries.tv

Graham Renouf
graham.john.renouf@gmail.com

Keith Taylor of Gilgal Ministries
www.crosst.org

Charles Walters of Walters Ministries
www.waltersministries.org

About the Author

RANDALL BURTON completed his ministerial studies at the Berean School of the Bible through the Assemblies of God. He is a graduate of Wagner Leadership Institute. Randall is co-founder and president of Zebulun Ministries Inc. He is the senior pastor of the multi-campus Northview Assembly of God Church in Columbus and Edinburgh, Indiana. He has a passion for revival, and Northview Church has been in a continuous move of God since 2011. Randall has been married to his wife, Cynthia, for 40 years. The Burtons have two sons and four granddaughters.

Contact Information

To book Randall Burton for speaking engagements or book signings or for more information,
call (812) 376-9749 or email at
northview2470@sbcglobal.net.

ENDNOTES

Chapter 1
[1]https://www.wthr.com/article/news/local/2008-flood-brings-permanent-changes-to-columbus/531-deaec75d-0bbf-4f88-b599-d8581b008f9f

[2]http://creationtoday.org/noahs-flood-points/

Chapter 2
[1]River Rising, Evergreen Press Pages 9 & 11

Chapter 6
[1]https://precepts.wordpress.com/2009/11/17/how-did-abraham-carry-the-fire/

Chapter 9
[1]https://www.worldatlas.com/rivers/10-most-famous-rivers-in-the-world.html

[2]More Holy Humor, From the best of the joyful newsletter, Cal and Rose Samra

Chapter 10
[1]https://www.merriam-webster.com/dictionary

[2]https://www.ausableriver.org/blog/why-do-streams-meander#:~:text=Meanders%20are%20produced%20when%20water,on%20subsequent%20inner%20bends%20downstream.

[3]https://www.theoi.com/Potamos/PotamosMaiandros.html

[4]https://www.theoi.com/Cult/PotamoiCult.html

[5]The Perry Stone Hebraic Prophetic Study Bible, King James Version. Copyright 2019 by Perry Stone.

Chapter 11
[1]https://banneroftruth.org/us/resources/articles/2009/the-beginning-of-the-1859-revival-in-ulster

[2]Seven Power Principles That I Didn't Learn in Seminary, C. Peter Wagner (Wagner Publications)

[1]https://www.defense.gov/News/Feature-Stories/story/Article/1650913/10-things-you-probably-didnt-know-about-the-pentagon

[2]Lincoln On Leadership (Executive Strategies For Tough Times) by Donald T. Phillips

Chapter 12
[1]https://www.facebook.com/166009616812256/posts/pfbid0VKc
wJnQq6wHbuqd1jHKC5ha9tfnvty7HRXuBYrN21cABnTknXasunTV
Dk9JNo7aRl

[2]https://greatawakening.blogspot.com/2012/03/100-year-old-
prophecies-of-revival

Made in the USA
Columbia, SC
16 February 2023

12478719R00055